A VICTORIAN VILLAGE

A Victorian Village

RALPH WHITLOCK

ROBERT HALE · LONDON

ISBN 0 7090 3897 6 (*cased edition*)
ISBN 0 7090 4516 6 (*paperback*)

Robert Hale Limited
Clerkenwell House
Clerkenwell Green
London EC1R 0HT

Photoset in North Wales by
Derek Doyle & Associates, Mold, Clwyd.
Printed in Great Britain by
St Edmundsbury Press, Bury St Edmunds, Suffolk.
Bound by WBC Bookbinders Limited.

Contents

Illustrations

PICTURE CREDITS

Chapter head illustrations, maps and jacket illustration by Roger Pearce. Chapter tail-pieces reproduced by permission of the *Western Gazette*, Yeovil, from the *Western Gazette Almanac* for 1906.

A Note on the Photographs

It should be remembered that the pioneering work on photography occurred in the 1830s and 1840s. It was not until the 1860s that ordinary villagers were able to have their photographs taken, generally on such special occasions as engagements and weddings. They were almost invariably posed photographs, staged in a studio.

Towards the end of the century photography moved outdoors, even into the villages, and it became quite fashionable for people to be photographed at the door of their home. But action photographs, of people actually doing something rather than posing, were still rare.

A parallel development in the last decades of the century was the magic lantern. The mass production of magic-lantern slides began in about 1870, and magic-lantern shows became popular entertainments in village halls and chapels. Those shown in the chapels were naturally of religious themes and, in true Victorian style, highly sentimental. In particular they were used extensively to propagate the Temperance movement, depicting in horrifying detail the evils of strong drink.

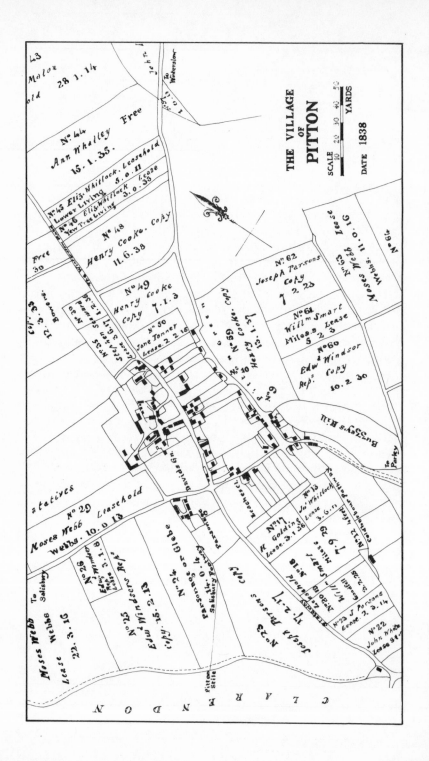

Preface:
An Explanatory Letter from the Author

This book is a sequel in reverse.

In *The Lost Village*, published in 1988, I set out to write a social study in depth of an English village between the two wars. It was a congenial project, for I was born and brought up in just such a village and so needed only to discuss a way of life that was entirely familiar to me. When the last chapter was written, however, there still seemed much to be said. Most of the questions which presented themselves were prefaced by 'Why?' The book described a community of small farms struggling in a mire of adversity. Why? Why were times so hard? Why were so many formerly productive fields lying derelict?

My father, Ted Whitlock, who was one of the principal characters of the book, had started his working life as a shepherd boy, and consequently there was much of shepherding lore, but why were there now hardly any sheep on the village farms? Why were the village farmers preferring to keep cows in a waterless valley clearly unsuited to dairying?

Ted's earliest reminiscences were of the menacing shadow of the workhouse. What was so terrifying about the workhouse? Faced with a minor mishap, such as the breaking of a tea-cup, his mother would sob, 'Oh dear! Now we shall all have to go to the workhouse!' Why?

Gleaning in the harvest fields featured prominently in his childhood memories. Why was gleaning so important? What was it, anyway? How did one set about it? What was killed with a silver gun? How did Winterslow Hut, nearly three miles from the village, fit into the picture? Why did villagers have to make secret nocturnal expeditions to the river banks at Alderbury to gather the dry, dead stalks of water dropwort?

Why did Ted not emigrate to Canada when he had the chance? And why was the opportunity offered him? Above all, why was there some doubt as to whether his father, Daniel, went to heaven?

My father, born in 1874, was married in 1901, but I, the eldest child of the family, was not born until 1914. So I was brought up in a household of adults well into middle age. Mealtime conversations tended to be about 'the old days'. I grew up as much at home in the Victorian era as in the post-war world. And over the past fifty years, by conversation and correspondence, I have accumulated voluminous files of information on the period.

When I settled down to write this book, however, it was not long before I realized that most of my information applied mostly to the last quarter of the nineteenth century, and that those twenty-five years were very different from the previous seventy-five. They were like the peaceful end of an autumn day, when the wild storms of the night and morning had blown themselves out. Autumn days of that sort, however, often end with frost. The gales subside, the lashing rain speeds away, and in the calm that follows the temperature plummets. After a brief period of noontide sunshine, an ordeal of a different nature develops. The villagers of Ted's generation were aware that they were living in a time of declining prosperity. The Golden Age of Victorian high farming had passed, for what reason they could not understand. Farmers carried on with practices that had served them well for decades and which they appreciated were fundamentally sound, and yet they went bankrupt. It was inexplicable.

So I perceived that it was necessary for me to go back farther, much farther, if I were to make sense of events in my father's lifetime. To find the answers to those 'Why?' questions I must investigate the earlier decades of the century, to penetrate even into the recesses of the eighteenth century.

Dark recesses. I found myself back in the days of Dickens and Oliver Twist. And even earlier, when boys of seven and eight were hanged for theft, when no fewer than two hundred offences were punishable by death. When a whole generation of peasants were made paupers by Acts of Parliament. When it seemed likely to some that France's bloody Revolution was about to be exported to Britain.

And I wanted this little history to be objective. History tends to be written by and for the winners – those who came off best. The villagers of my Victorian village were mostly losers. In mid-century the village comprised about a hundred houses. Its population was about 400. Of these not more than fifty were farmers, builders, carpenters, other craftsmen and artisans, together with an innkeeper, a parson and a few other anomalous characters. All the others were classified as agricultural labourers. At least, that was their status in 1850. It was otherwise in 1800. Then many of them, probably most of them, had been independent peasants, each with his cottage and paddock, his cultivated strips in the open fields and his rights on the common land. His lot in life had deteriorated, and he knew it.

It was about this submerged class that I had to write, primarily because of their numerical preponderance but also because that is where I, like most other people who push back family history research far enough, belonged. My paternal grandmother, losing her husband, an agricultural labourer, had to rear her three small children on a pauper allowance of 5 shillings a week and two loaves of workhouse bread ...

In the end I found answers to all my questions, to my satisfaction and, I hope, to my readers' too. Not excepting the metaphysical conundrum, Did Grandfather Daniel land safely in heaven after all?

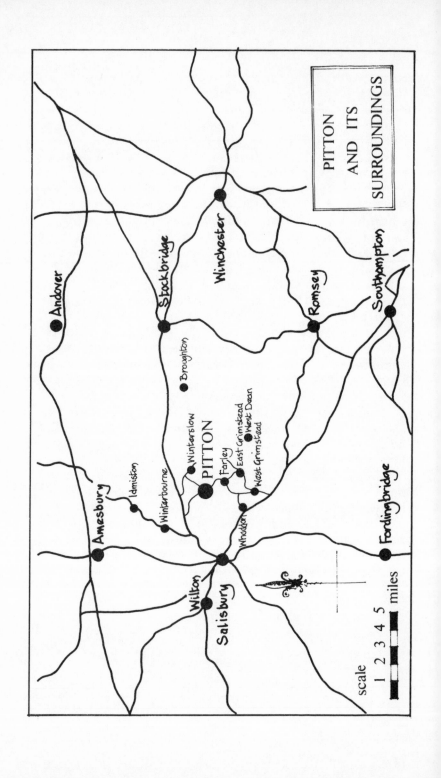

PITTON
AND ITS
SURROUNDINGS

Andover

Stockbridge

Winchester

Romsey

Southampton

Broughton

Winterslow

East Grimstead
West Dean

PITTON

Farley

West Grimstead

Idmiston

Amesbury

Winterbourne

Whaddon

Fordingbridge

Wilton

Salisbury

scale
1 2 3 4 5
miles

1 The Dry Ditch

The three horsemen were conversing under an oak in a little hedged meadow between Pitton and Farley on this tenth day of October 1651. Yeoman farmers, one would have said. One of them, a stocky young man with short-cropped fair hair, would, under the circumstances, have answered that description. Stephen Fox was here on his home ground.

A Farley man of good peasant stock (his father was William Fox, his mother a Pavey, his grandmother a Whitlock – all well-established local names), Stephen had been more fortunate than most of his contemporaries. A somewhat precocious lad, with a penchant for mathematics, he had been given, by a donor now unknown, an education at the Cathedral School at Salisbury. His patron had also presumably been responsible for securing for him a post in the household of the Earl of Newcastle, a courtier in high favour with Charles I in happier days. Indeed, the King had appointed Newcastle governor to his small son, the future Charles II. So, as a member of Newcastle's retinue, Stephen Fox was soon deeply involved in Court matters, though in a humble capacity. The earl was the courtier *par excellence*, a superb horseman, fond of dancing and fencing, enjoying music, poetry and the theatre, and highly popular with his contemporaries. Stephen could not have had a better introduction to his future career.

Now circumstances were reversed. Fox was back at home; Charles was a fugitive. Since the disastrous defeat at the Battle of Worcester on 3 September Charles had been a hunted man, a price of £1,000 (then a colossal sum) on his head. After the escapade of the Boscobel Oak he had dodged hither and thither across England, accompanied by only a few friends and attendants. A description of him had been widely circulated – 'a tall black man, over two yards high'. (His height was, in fact, six feet two inches.)

First they had attempted to make for a Welsh port, in their search for a ship to take them to the Continent. Foiled, they tried Bristol but could not make contact with a reliable shipmaster. At Trent, near Sherborne in north Dorset, the home of Colonel Francis Wyndham had offered a fairly safe temporary refuge, and Charles arrived there on 22 September. It seemed an ideal base from which to plan an escape across the Channel via one of the little Dorset ports, but, as luck would have it, those ports were brimful of Commonwealth soldiers, embarking for a campaign in Jersey, one of the last Royalist strongholds.

After sundry hair-raising adventures, the party decided to move farther east, even though that took them nearer the danger zone of London. On 6 October they moved base to Heale House, six miles north of Salisbury, where a loyal household provided hospitality for the next eight days.

At nights Charles slept in a hidey-hole, constructed for Catholic priests, as at Trent Manor, but by day he went out riding, on sightseeing excursions. One expedition was to Stonehenge where, as he told Pepys, 'We stayed looking at the stones for some time.' Another was evidently to Farley, some eight miles across country from Heale House. His contact there was doubtless Stephen Fox, who reported that Southampton was too dangerous to be considered as a port of embarkation, being, like Lyme and Bridport, full of Parliamentary troops bound for Jersey. It was eventually decided to look farther east, to the ports of Sussex.

Throughout these adventures Charles was suitably

disguised. Soon after his escape from Worcester he had changed his clothes (and had his own thrown into a 'privvy-house') and was dressed as a yeoman, in 'a green jerkin, grey cloth breeches, leather doublet and greasy soft hat'. His luxuriant black hair was cropped short, and his face and hands were stained with walnut juice. Unhappily for his comfort, the clothes he borrowed were those of a giant of a man, William Penderel, whose boots were so large that they chafed Charles's feet badly, even when stuffed with paper. Charles's unusual height and gait (he had a long, loping stride) could hardly be disguised, though when he was mounted on a nag of the type common on farms of that time they were not quite so noticeable.

Now, in the Farley meadow, Stephen Fox was bringing the latest news of negotiations for cross-Channel ferrying. There had been encouraging responses from Brighthelmstone (now Brighton), and Charles was eventually able to embark at nearby Shoreham Harbour. For both Stephen and Charles it was a meeting of old acquaintances, and the King had every reason to rely on his loyalty. Which was about to be put to the test.

The third member of the party was an undisguised Cavalier, a handsome man of arrogant bearing, still flaunting his long, curled locks. In keeping with his role of country landowner, he rode a better horse than the other two, Charles playing the part of his servant. He was Lord Wilmot, who had been with the King from the very beginning of the flight and had, in fact, been more or less in charge of operations.

It was he who caught the distant clip-clop of horses' hooves on a flinty road, far off but approaching. It could only be a party of Parliamentary troopers: the King had now no men under arms. He broke into the conversation.

'Listen!'

There was no mistaking the ominous sounds. Stephen was equal to the occasion.

'Quick! Off the horses!'

Seizing the reins of the other two horses, he led them towards the cover of the woods (now Hound Wood).

'Get into the ditch,' he called back.

The ditch was fortunately a dry one – one of the sort devised as an adjunct to a cattle-proof boundary fence. It ran alongside a stout hedge which, farther along, two men were trimming with bill-hooks. The King looked at them askance.

'What of these?'

'Never fear,' Stephen assured him. 'They're my kinsmen. They'll not betray you.'

With Stephen hastening towards the anonymity of the wood, Charles and Wilmot scrambled into the ditch. The hedgers continued with their work and obligingly arranged a few casual branches and twigs to help conceal them. When a dozen or so Commonwealth mounted soldiers, cantering up the lane, came across to interrogate them, they said, 'Yes, we saw three horsemen a short time ago. They went in that direction,' pointing westwards to Clarendon, the opposite to that taken by Stephen.

When it was safe, the fugitives crawled out of the ditch and trudged off down to Farley, where they found their horses in the stables of Stephen's father.

Just another adventure, an episode in the dramatic saga of the King's flight. It has been considered hardly worth a mention in any surviving records of the period. It was remembered locally, though. Three hundred years later the villagers of Farley and Pitton knew that once King Charles had come riding that way and had escaped from his enemies by hiding in a ditch. They did not know which ditch it was, and there are plenty in the vicinity. A clue, however, does exist.

Among the long-established agricultural holdings in Pitton is one with a very curious composition. It consists of a house with farmyard buildings, orchard and paddock in the middle of the village, together with a block of about forty acres of arable land half a mile or so along the road leading to Winterslow, and two little meadows of some two acres each, about midway between Pitton and Farley. A decidedly awkward unit to farm, yet it has endured, intact, for over 250 years. The present owner has, within the past thirty years, sold the property in the middle of the village but retains, as his farm, the two parcels of land more than a mile apart. His name is Stephen Whitlock.

And the land has been farmed by Whitlocks, though mostly as tenants, for all those years.

The two little meadows between Pitton and Farley bear a significant name, Wilmot's.

After Charles's restoration to the throne, did he remember to reward those loyal peasants who had unhesitatingly turned down a reward for his capture that represented more than they could have earned by a lifetime of hard work? Did he entrust their welfare to Lord Wilmot, who then bought the land and made them tenants in perpetuity? It would be in keeping with Charles's known generosity to those who helped him in his adversity.

Or is it just coincidence that the field should bear that name? No one knows. At some time in the eighteenth century a Salisbury tradesman named Wilmot is involved in some way, but we have no means of knowing whether he was a descendant of the Wilmot who was the Earl of Rochester. Whoever he was, the Whitlocks were still his tenants.

It is only right to add that a Winterslow tradition has a different identification of the ditch in which Charles hid. It places it as 'Dean Hedge, between The Livery and Farley'.

Ditching

2   The Setting

Salisbury Plain is like the sea. Before it was invaded by the plough, its undulating turf, fading to grey-blue with distance, resembled the petrified waves of some immense ocean. The beech-crowned hilltops were atolls, bravely surveying the heaving waters. The blue-rinsed clouds, detaching themselves from the blue horizon and sailing unhurriedly across the zenith, must necessarily have their birth in the blue sea.

An undulating plateau, the Plain tilts gently from north-west to south-east and is very roughly circular, with a diameter of from thirty to forty miles. Its altitude ranges from about 120 feet to 945 feet above sea-level, but its more general limits are between 250 feet in the valley bottoms to 400 or 500 feet on the hills. This chalk land is drained by five rivers, which on the map appear to fan out from Salisbury like the fingers of a hand. They are fed by deep and sometimes narrow tributary valleys which penetrate into the heart of the downs and which are waterless except between December and March, when some of them have temporary clear streams, known as winterbournes.

Another feature of the Plain increases its resemblance to the sea. Many of its undulations are smooth and gentle, like the drowsy swell of the ocean on a sunny summer day, but in certain sectors the hills heave up like waves and poise, on the point of breaking, on the edge of some defenceless valley.

Among the most spectacular of these scarps are those hanging over the Wylye and Chalke valleys and the one which marks the northern boundary of the Plain. Another, clearly demarcated but not quite as impressive, represents the south-eastern frontier. It is this one which marks the scene of our book.

A motorist speeding westwards along the A30 picks it up on his left soon after leaving Stockbridge. It provides his southern horizon until he passes the Pheasant Inn, where the road begins to veer gradually to the right, to ensure that it doesn't miss Salisbury. If he were to take a by-road to the left, a few hundred yards past the Pheasant, he would, within a couple of miles, arrive at Pitton, whose story throughout the nineteenth century is about to be unfolded.

To the question 'Why is Pitton situated where it is?', no clear answer is forthcoming. Over the downs to the north are dozens of valleys, empty of settlements, which would seem to be equally suitable. Less than two miles to the north is an almost identical parallel valley occupied by just three farms apparently of medieval origin, which is no great age in the venerable history of Wessex. The likeliest explanation is that there is a link with Aymer's Pond, in the floor of the valley within a few yards of the church. Bearing in mind that the water table in much of the chalk downland country of Wessex is estimated to have fallen at least 150 feet since Roman times (and probably more than that now, with the greatly increased demand for water during the past half-century), Aymer's Pond, now dry, was probably a permanent pool in early times. In an otherwise waterless countryside, it could well have been regarded as a sacred pool.

Nearly all the villages in these parts bear Anglo-Saxon names. 'Pitton' is derived from the Saxon word for a hawk. Possibly it was founded by a man, Putta, whose name meant 'the Hawk'; or perhaps it was a place where hawks were kept. Pitton's neighbour just over the hill, Farley, simply means 'far meadow'. Winterslow, which features in our story, was the home of an Anglo-Saxon named

Wintra. Then there are Alderbury, where Alward lived, and Whaddon – 'wheat down', and the two Grimsteads, commemorating a character, Grim, and Dean, a name which survives in modern English as denoting 'a narrow wooded valley with a stream', an exact description of the site of the village.

Yet most of the village sites were well populated long before Anglo-Saxon times. Winterslow, which sits astride the Roman road from Old Sarum (Sorbiodunum) to Winchester (Venta Belgarum) has at least one Roman farm site. Silva Strata ('road through the woods') is said to have been the Roman name for the oldest road in Alderbury, now known as Silver Street. It leads down a steep hill to a ford across the River Avon – the Long Ford. The railway station at West Dean occupies part of the site of a Roman villa which, by its very size, must have been the administrative headquarters of a large agricultural estate.

And all around the district are evidences of still earlier inhabitants. The great Iron Age hill-fort of Danebury, which flourished in the first millennium BC, is only about eight miles away to the east. Flint mines dating from about 1600 BC have been excavated on Easton Down, Winterslow. Near the Pheasant Inn, Winterslow, is the site of a bell barrow, dating from about 1000 BC, which yielded some remarkable artefacts when excavated early in the nineteenth century. The skeleton of a man who died about 1500 BC has been unearthed actually within Pitton village, while between Pitton and Winterslow is a long barrow of perhaps 2500 BC.

During the Roman era Celtic peasants inhabited a village on the downs about a mile north-west of Pitton. Its site has not yet been excavated, but its graveyard has, and has yielded a good deal of fascinating material. The villagers were poor but not slaves. They wore boots and were buried (except for a few cremations) in coffins fashioned with the minimum number of iron nails. One skeleton was of an old lady crippled with arthritis, who had evidently been fed and cared for years after she was a working member of the community. Or perhaps she was a witch!

Coins show that the village flourished until some time

after AD 363, when Roman Britain was subjected to a devastating invasion by Irish and Saxon freebooters. Night descended on civilization in Britain, and only brief glimmers of illumination are thrown on the scene for several centuries. According to the *Anglo-Saxon Chronicle*, a free Romano-British population survived until the year 552, when invading Saxons defeated them near Old Sarum. Until that time Amesbury, about eight miles to the north of Pitton, was the home of one of the Three Perpetual Choirs of Britain, where relays of monks praised God day and night without ceasing.

It is generally agreed that the Anglo-Saxon invaders penetrated the country primarily along the river valleys, as the Anglo-Saxon names of the strings of villages along the rivers around Salisbury confirm. Winterslow, however, was an exception. As far as can be ascertained, the village site continued to be occupied all through those Dark Ages. Perhaps from its hilltop a garrison guarded the old Roman highway which gave access to the heartland of Wessex. If so, the hillside fields around would have been cultivated as they had been in Roman times. The sacred pool in the Pitton valley could well have been a place of worship for the entire surviving population of the district, and eventually the site for a permanent settlement.

All is conjecture, but a few clues suggest that it is on the right lines. The site of Pitton church is a slightly raised circular enclosure on the edge of the pond. At least, it was circular to within the memory of villagers alive in the 1920s, who remembered when slices were carved out of it to enlarge neighbouring properties. When in the 1830s the village Methodists wanted to build a chapel, to replace the cottage in which they had been meeting, the site that a local farmer gave them was as near the church as possible. The two congregations must have been able to hear each other singing! Evidently the site retained some special significance.

Perhaps even more suggestive was the attitude of the natives of Pitton to their immediate neighbours.

'We marries wi' Winterslow,' one old man asserted. 'We don't have owt to do wi' they Farley jiggers.'

It wasn't true. Examination of the records reveals

frequent intermarriages with both villages. But in the mind of the old man, and of many others still remembered, was a tradition that the affinities of Pitton were with Winterslow, not with Farley, even though from 1874 onwards Pitton and Farley were one parish.

One can reconstruct the likely sequence of events. The Saxon invaders came in their ships up the Avon to the Long Ford, where, under a leader named Aylward, they disembarked and founded the village of Aylward's-bury. From there over the succeeding decades, perhaps centuries, they spread out, penetrating the dense forest and founding new settlements – Whaddon, Clarendon, the Grimsteads and, finally, Farley, 'the far meadow'. But when they attempted to expand still farther, they found their way blocked by the existing settlements of Pitton and Winterslow. Hence the enduring antipathy, dimly remembered long after the reasons had been forgotten.

It surfaced again in the late seventeenth century, when that illustrious native of Farley Sir Stephen Fox decided to give his home village a new church. He enlisted the co-operation of his friend Sir Christopher Wren, and Farley's Church of All Saints is often supposed to be a Wren church, though informed opinion is that it is the work of one of Sir Christopher's assistants. The attitude of the contemporary Farley villagers to their splendid new church is revealing. They rejoiced not so much at the fine architecture and imposing interior but that, in lieu of their 'ancient ruined chapel', they now possessed a church *bigger* than that of their detested neighbours at Pitton!

3   Before Shops

Whatever the sequence of events that established Pitton in its valley, the overriding factor in deciding whether the settlement would be permanent was the fertility of the surrounding fields. And that has been the justification for its continued existence ever since – at least until its suburbanization by the arrival of commuters in the middle of the present century. Until then Pitton, like more than 9,000 other English villages, was or had the potential to be more or less self-sufficient in food. In earlier centuries the villagers had also to rely on their own resources for clothes, fabrics in general, fuel, building material, containers, tools and such commodities as soap and medicine.

The theme of this book is the opening of new horizons for country-dwellers, the peasantry, in the nineteenth century. Though the village of the period between the two world wars of the present century, as portrayed in my book *The Lost Village*, was by modern standards exceedingly in-growing and parochial, it was, in fact, a vastly improved and enlightened community compared with that of the year 1800. A chronicler at the beginning of certain (though not all) previous centuries might have made a similar claim.

It may therefore be helpful, in appreciating the significance of events dealt with in this book, to look at a rural community which was as near self-sufficient as any could be. Rather than journeying some 10,000 miles to study a primitive tribe in Amazonia or New Guinea, we will step back 2,000 years to visit the Iron Age hill-fort of Danebury in Hampshire. It has the advantage of being situated less than ten miles from Pitton, making it probable that if Pitton existed in those days the two communities would have been aware of each other.

Dr Barry Cunliffe, a former colleague of the author, who conducted intensive excavations at the site in the 1970s, gives in his book *Danebury* a graphic picture of life in this self-sufficient community. Its population is estimated at between 250 and 300, which is a little less than that of Pitton in the nineteenth century. There were in addition numerous satellite farms, though on what terms they were associated with the central settlement is not known. It has been asserted that a person walking along a main highway or even a country road at the peak of the Roman era would have passed a farmstead, villa or some sort of human habitation every few hundred yards, and the population was probably not much less dense in Celtic times.

The inhabitants of Danebury and its farms had a diet primarily of cereals, reinforced quite frequently by meat. They grew wheat and barley and, to judge from the number of storage pits and granaries, produced a considerable surplus. They kept sheep, cattle and pigs, also dogs and perhaps a few goats. Apparently they made hay for winter fodder for their ruminant animals, though it is suggested that some of the barley may have been cut unripe and stored in ricks for cattle food. The sheep were kept primarily for their wool, which was probably combed out rather than shorn. Spinning and weaving were essentially cottage industries, in the sense that they were carried out within the walls of the settlement. Cows were multi-purpose stock, though they seem to have been valued chiefly as draught animals. No doubt they were milked for the few pints they were capable of producing, but the comparative absence on the site of the bones of young cattle seems to imply that the cows were killed off only when they were too old for work. Dead, they yielded not only meat but hides, harness, thongs, leather for buckets, footwear and other clothes, and sinews for sewing and perhaps for weaponry. They were also in all probability used as a form of currency or barter.

Timber for building and the making of tools was available in abundance. Many of the buildings had beaten chalk floors, and chalk cob was probably much used for walls. Of equal importance in house construction was wattlework, mostly of hazel, which was coppiced in a manner entirely familiar to the villagers of 2,000 years later. For outer walls the wattlework was plastered with clay, and clay was, of course, in much demand for pottery. Osiers were employed for basketwork, and rushes for mats. Some of the thatch for houses and barns may have come from wheat straw, but the more durable reeds from the River Test, not far away, are a more likely material. Any illumination was probably provided by tallow candles or torches.

The only important essentials missing were metals, stone and salt. At this date iron ore was being mined in The Weald, in north Wiltshire and at Hengistbury Head (at the entrance to Christchurch Harbour). As it was evidently scarce and valuable, every bit of iron was retained and reused time and again, and the smiths of Danebury were demonstrably highly skilled. Bars of iron were also being used as currency. Stone was needed for querns, for grinding corn, and also for whetstones. At Danebury numerous stone weights were found. The salt used was sea-salt, from the Dorset coast.

A Pitton peasant of the year 1800 would have felt reasonably at home in the Danebury of 2,000 years earlier. His social superiors would have noticed a lack of comfort and would have deplored the barbarity of manners and the illiteracy of the Celtic aristocracy, but he himself would have found the basic essentials of life he was used to and would have fitted into the daily scheme of things without overmuch adjustment.

Let us identify him, this Pitton peasant of the year 1800. It is not difficult, for we find him, as a man aged seventy-one, in the 1851 census (a revealing document to which we shall be returning later). He is described as an agricultural labourer and a widower, living alone. 'Collins' is an old Pitton name, borne by eleven other heads of families, with a total score of twenty-five children between them. So in 1800 he would have been aged twenty and probably on the threshold of getting married. No doubt some of the many other Collinses of 1851 were his descendants.

We have no means of knowing just where in the village his cottage stood, except that it was not by The Green, Cold Harbour or Slateway, for houses in those areas are mentioned specifically in the census. In all probability it was a cottage which has long since disappeared. To judge from cottages which survived into the twentieth century, it would have been a modest cob-walled building, roofed with thatch and with a beaten chalk floor. In fact, it would have been very similar to the Danebury cottages of 2,000 years earlier, except that they were round, whereas the Pitton version was rectangular. John Collins' cottage may have been one of a pair, with one room upstairs and one down, with a lean-to at the back, or it may simply have had two rooms at ground level.

It would, however, have been set in a fairly spacious, hedged garden, reminiscent of the days of Good Queen Bess, when an enactment required that every new cottage built to have at least an acre or two of land, that being considered the minimum required for a man to support himself and his family and so to be assured of not requiring help from the parish. For although John Collins may have been an agricultural labourer in his old age in 1851, he need not have been in 1800. It is true that there were farm labourers, wholly employed by some of the larger farmers, in 1800, but most of the villagers were independent peasants, busy on their own little holdings for much of the time, though glad to undertake part-time seasonal work for their larger neighbours at haymaking and harvest. 'Husbandmen' they were referred to in eighteenth-century parish registers. By the early years of this century they were 'smallholders'.

The impact of the Enclosure Acts (to be considered in our next chapter) did not hit Pitton and Farley until 1819. Until that date the old open-field system, worked out painfully over the preceding centuries, still prevailed.

Technically inefficient and a brake on agricultural progress, it nevertheless produced and perpetuated an admirable social system the shattering of which caused great hardship.

The open-field system had arisen from the gradual realization that soil would not produce crops indefinitely without having its fertility replenished by some method or another. There is evidence that the inhabitants of Danebury had discovered this. In the later phases of occupation a discernible increase in the numbers of sheep, at the expense of cattle, occurred, and the archaeologists interpret this as indicating that sheep, penned in hurdle enclosures, were being used to manure the fields with their droppings. An early example of the principle of 'the golden hoof', on which Victorian 'high farming' was based.

Our Anglo-Saxon ancestors, when they arrived as settlers, had to learn this lesson afresh. Arriving in a plundered and neglected countryside, they settled wherever cultivation was easy and opposition negligible, cultivated the land for a few years and then, when yields began to fall, moved on. As the settlers became more and more numerous, however, that option became closed. From being semi-nomadic they had necessarily to become sedentary, as has happened in so many Third World countries in the present century.

The system they devised to counteract declining fertility of the soil was to give each field a rest every third year. In the first year it grew wheat; in the second year, barley; and in the third it lay fallow. Oats were in some districts grown instead of barley, but not at the expense of introducing an extra year of cereal-growing, for the aim was to get back to the supremely important wheat as quickly as possible. By John Collins' time 'fallow' had come to imply a thorough cleaning of the land by frequent ploughing, harrowing and operations to destroy weeds during the summer months. John would have known the maxim that, 'A summer's exposure to sunlight and air did the soil as much good as a coat of manure.' In earlier times, however, 'fallow' meant a mere rest for exhausted soil. A fallow field was allowed to grow weeds, including of course many indigenous grasses, which were grazed by the village livestock. This method gave the land a modest application of manure but contributed nothing at all to the suppression of weeds.

By 1800 an additional crop had been introduced on many Wiltshire farms. After barley a crop of clover or of turnips was interposed, thus creating a four-course rotation. Either crop was grazed by closely folded sheep, which gave the soil a rich coating of dung, so restoring a technique practised at Danebury long before the Roman invasion. John Collins during his years as a farm labourer would probably have spent many summers hoeing, by hand-hoe, fields of turnips.

Anglo-Saxon settlements came to follow a fairly stereotyped pattern. The cultivable land around each was divided into three great fields, which were in turn subdivided among the settlers, each according to his status. The standard land-measurement was the *hide*, which was roughly the amount of land which could be ploughed by an eight-ox team in a year. It naturally varied from district to district, according to the stiffness of the soil, but seems to have averaged about 120 acres. Not many settlers owned an eight-ox team, and not many were entitled to a full hide of land, though the head of the settlement – a thane in Anglo-Saxon times, a lord of the manor in later centuries – might be allocated a number of hides.

Most of the original Anglo-Saxon settlers were free peasants who had willingly followed their leader from their Scandinavian homeland to the new country overseas. Collectively they were known as *ceorls*, which in later times their Norman overlords referred to derogatively as 'churls'. Like the land, they were divided into categories. A completely free peasant was known as a *geneat* or 'villein'. He was entitled to a 'virgate' of land – a quarter of a hide and therefore about thirty acres. A step lower in the social scale was the *gebur* or 'bordar', whose holding was a 'bovate' (about fifteen acres). He normally owned just one ox. A *colibert* or *cosetle* or 'cottar' had no ox and so had to cultivate his five acres by spade and hoe. He was often a freed serf. Finally, there were 'serfs', who were in effect slaves. They were tied to the land and were expected to work for no wages, but they had certain basic rights and were allotted an acre each for their maintenance.

All these classes were, however, regarded as tenants, owing allegiance to their thane or lord of the manor. Theoretically, they should have paid rent to him, but as theirs was an economy in which cash played a relatively minor part, they discharged their obligations by a stipulated amount of work on the lord's farm.

The Anglo-Saxon settlers possessed a strong notion of fair play. They accepted that there had to be a class structure, but within it everyone had to have a fair chance of livelihood. It would never do, for instance, for one man to have all the best land in the settlement while another had to make do with some of the worst. For this reason each of the three great fields was subdivided into one-acre segments.

The Anglo-Saxon plough was a cumbersome tool, and using it with an eight-ox team, two oxen abreast, called for the exercise of considerable skill on the part of the ploughman. In particular, he ploughed a furrow as long as possible before embarking on the tricky business of turning. The subdivisions of the great fields were thus long, narrow strips. In the course of the centuries they became standardized.

In his primary schooldays, in the early 1920s, the author learned to recite the old English land-measurement tables:

12 inches = 1 foot
3 feet = 1 yard
5½ yards = 1 rod, pole or perch
4 rods, poles or perches = 1 chain
10 chains = 1 furlong
8 furlongs = 1 mile

It has little or no application today, except that one chain, twenty-two yards, is the length of a cricket pitch!

In early times, a strip field one furlong long by one chain broad (220 yards by twenty-two yards) was an acre (4,840 square yards) and was regarded as a good day's ploughing for that eight-ox team. Incidentally, the square rod, pole or perch was also a much-used measurement,

known in Wiltshire as a 'lug'. A householder would refer
to his garden extending to so many lugs, or he would
agree to rent so many lugs of allotment. Most villagers
could estimate pretty accurately, by eye, the size of a plot
of land, in lugs.

So then the Anglo-Saxon villein would have his
thirty-acre holding consisting of thirty separate acre strips
in the great open fields. To make matters fairer still, it was
held that the strips should not be contiguous, and in some
manors there was an annual re-allocation of strips, which
had the obvious disadvantage that no man had any
incentive to improve his acres.

The open fields of Pitton extended to the north,
north-west and north-east of the village, with a smaller
area farther down the valley, to the south. On the far slope
of the steep hill which hides the village from the rising sun
is an area marked on the oldest maps as 'Ancient
Enclosures'. On the accepted principle that the age of a
hedge may be determined by the number of species of
trees or bushes in it, these enclosures must have been
made in the eleventh century, soon after the time of
William the Conqueror. Their enclosing hedges today are
formed of hazel, oak, hawthorn, blackthorn, holly, briar,
bramble and maple. (Whether bramble should be included
seems doubtful, but there are also a few bushes of elder
and dogwood and in places some ash, so if there is any
error, it is on the conservative side.) Incidentally, although
many of the hedges have now disappeared, within living
memory and certainly at the beginning of the nineteenth
century the whole area was a network of little fields, each
an acre in extent. Each of the village farmers had his strips
in the open fields and also one or two hedged fields in the
'ancient enclosures'. The incentive for these enclosures
seems to have been to give each of the farmers access to
hazel and other underwood from which he could cut his
own hurdles, fencing stakes, thatching spars and other
requisites.

In addition to their open fields most Anglo-Saxon
settlements possessed an area, often very extensive, of
land held in common. Usually it was land difficult to
plough, by reason of being too wet, too stony or densely

clothed in trees. It could also be land surplus to the requirements of the original settlers and afterwards left undisturbed to fit in with the concept of common land.

To the east of Pitton, adjoining the 'ancient enclosures' and linking up with the grassy hill which overshadows the village, was an area known to John Collins as Pitton Down. Its northern boundary was the lane now known as Winterslow Hollow but formerly the main road to Winterslow; its southern frontier is shared with the present Hound Wood, which John Collins knew as Cobblers Copse and Church Copse. It was chalk pasture, typical of the immense grasslands of Salisbury Plain, stretching away to the north, and it had an important role in the village economy, for the village livestock, like the village land, was allocated to the villagers according to social status. The livestock of the community had to be strictly controlled, in some way or another, to avoid overstocking. Apart from the garden or paddock around his house and buildings, a householder had no fenced ground of his own. He was, however, entitled to run a specified number of animals on the common land. The custom is still observed on a number of surviving commons, notably in the New Forest, where the rights are attached to the holding, not to persons. Probably the same rule applied to Pitton.

The livestock thus regulated were mainly cattle and sheep. Geese also roamed the common, in the charge of a goose-girl, but pigs were, as a rule, regarded as entirely forest animals, where their rooting would not spoil the grazing for other animals. Although Pitton was, to a considerable extent, a forest village, many of its inhabitants deriving their livelihood from work in the woods, the woods in question were those of the Clarendon Estate, on the far side of the parish boundary and therefore beyond the scope of common rights.

Thomas Davis of Longleat (on the far side of Wiltshire from Pitton) has left us a valuable account of farming in the county in his day. His book *A General View of the Agriculture of Wiltshire* was published by the then new Board of Agriculture in 1811, but it was based largely on material collected by his father in 1794. Enclosures were then proceeding at a rapid pace, but Davis estimated that about a quarter of the farmland of the county was still common land, and he was therefore quite familiar with the system.

He differentiates between sheep commons and cow commons, the former being by far the more numerous in Wiltshire. 'The common sheep-down,' he writes, 'is open for the common flocks during the summer and autumn. The unsown or summer-field [he means the fallow] is also open till it is ploughed for wheat; after that the sheep have only the down till the harvest is over. When the corn fields are clear, the flock has those fields and the down till the winter obliges the owners to give them hay.'

Now comes a reference to an important character in the village scene – the common shepherd. Evidently it was ancient practice to entrust all the sheep of the manor, regardless of ownership, to the care of a chief shepherd. Davis, however, notes that, since the value of sheep had become more widely appreciated, 'The tenants of common fields have introduced the practice of folding their separate flocks on their own lands, thereby placing their sheep under the immediate care of their own servants, rather than entrusting them to a common shepherd, *whose neglect or partiality made his attentions inadequate.*' Prior to the change, when winter began, 'Every commoner finds his own fold and his own hay, but the common shepherd feeds and folds the whole.'

The common shepherd was heir to a venerable tradition. In medieval times, when sheep were commonly milked, he had the duty of milking all the ewes twice a day and of making butter and cheese. For his services he was entitled to a lamb and a fleece annually, all the milk from the entire flock for seven nights after midsummer, and a bowl of whey every evening in summer. For twelve nights in midwinter, presumably the Twelve Nights of Christmas, he also had the right to pen the sheep on his own land – a provision which implies that he was a peasant with a few strips in the open fields and also that the value of sheep manure was well appreciated.

The cowherd was of the same status as the shepherd, though cows in this part of southern England were much less numerous than sheep. They needed better grazing than the sheep, as well as easy access to water. Says Davis, 'The common herd of cows begin to feed the cow downs early in May, usually Holyrood-day, and finished when the fields are clear of corn ... When the stubble-fields are open the cows have a right to feed them jointly with the sheep, and if there are common meadows they have an exclusive right to feed them till the end of the commoning season, usually St Martin's-day, November 11th, O.S., when the owners take them home to the straw-yards.'

The cowherd too had his perquisites. They included the milk from each heifer for fourteen days after calving and from each old cow for seven days after calving. The cows were milked twice a day, three times a day in May, but the cowherd did not make butter or cheese. He had to hand the milk over to another specialist, the cheese-maker, a woman. She was usually on the staff of the lord of the manor but was allowed to keep for herself the whey or buttermilk and also the curds strained from the cheese. From these she made butter, as some farmhouse cheese-makers still do today.

The oxherd, who had care of the draught oxen, was distinct from the cowherd. He was a night-shift worker, taking charge of the oxen after they had finished their day's work in the fields and guarding them, either at pasture or, in winter, in stalls all night. He had to ensure that they were fed and watered before the ploughmen called for them in the morning. Caedmon, the first English poet of whom we have any knowledge (he died in about 680), was an oxherd. He composed his great poem in the ox-stall one winter night, after returning from a party in a neighbour's house.

The swineherd was definitely a share-cropper. All the pigs on the manor were committed to his charge, and his payment was a proportion of all the young pigs born. Although the woodlands attached to a parish or manor were subject to common rights, they belonged theoretically to the lord of the manor, who could claim a proportion of all the pigs turned loose by his tenants. The season of pannage (foraging rights for pigs in the woods) was for two or three months in autumn, during which period the pigs grew fat on acorns and roots. A holocaust of all the surplus stock then occurred, and, after the initial feast, the carcases were salted down or otherwise preserved for winter use.

One provision, which dates back to at least the time of Alfred the Great, strikes us as being surprisingly modern, for it introduces a standard criterion of quality which is still widely used today. At the time of slaughter the back fat was measured. The lord of the manor could claim one-third of those pigs which had accumulated, presumably from feeding on his acorns and beechmast, back fat of three fingers thickness. From those whose back fat was the thickness of two fingers, he was entitled to a quarter, and from those with a back fat thickness of a thumb, he took one-fifth. Nowadays the back-fat thickness is measured electronically, on living pigs.

The swineherd was also the parish pig-killer. He was skilled in dressing and curing as well as in killing pigs. For his services in this respect he was entitled to the chitterlings and some of the other offal from each pig. In the early years of the twentieth century the author's father, who was then regarded as the village pig-killer, could claim similar perquisites. Even here, however, there was a further subdivision of privileges and responsibilities. When Ted Whitlock arrived at a neighbour's to kill a pig, Lizzie Collins, a spinster lady of uncertain age, was sure to be there with a bucket, to catch the blood for making black puddings, which she claimed as her right.

Horses, after they had declined during the Middle Ages to the humble status of farm animals, shared the common grazing with cows, oxen and sheep and had no specialist warden to look after their interest.

The picture that thus emerges of Pitton at the beginning of the nineteenth century is of a virtually self-sufficient and carefully regulated community, managing its affairs in accordance with age-old custom. The details of the management of sheep rights and cow rights on commons, in strict relation to the calendar, and the measurement of back fat in pigs (as already quoted) illustrate how minutely the rules had been evolved in the course of centuries. A system theoretically fairer would have been hard to devise, though, human nature being what it is, abuses doubtless crept in.

Specialists, such as the blacksmith and the thatcher, possessed their own little holdings, in addition to their income from the practice of their craft. Each would have a number of arable strips in the open fields and grazing rights on the common land. Not too many rights, of course, or that would have prejudiced their main role in the village economy, but they would have enough corn land to keep their family in bread and enough common rights to enable them to pasture a house cow or two and perhaps a few sheep.

An example of how the system worked for an individual is provided by the story of Elisha Whitlock, who survived, operating under more or less the old rules, until towards the end of the nineteenth century. It has been given in *The Lost Village* but will bear a brief repetition here.

Long before then, of course, the open fields had been enclosed, as we shall see in the next chapter, but Elisha had managed to hang on to his allocation of land at the enclosure award. It happened to be two little fields, probably less than four acres in extent, at the top of Dunley Hill, a good mile from his home in Sinnetts Close, on the far side of the village. There he lived in a cob-and-thatch cottage flanked by a muddy yard and a back paddock and a small orchard, the whole property amounting to less than an acre. Theoretically, however, and in his own opinion, he was a farmer. He kept three cows, about a dozen hens and an equal number of cockerels, a pig and three geese.

The two little fields, awarded in lieu of four strips in the open fields at the time of the enclosure, were too small and too shaded by broad hedges for ploughing, but it suited Elisha very well to keep them as meadows. Every morning, after milking and feeding his other livestock, he took his cows through the village and down the long lane of Slateway to their pasture. He didn't hurry, for Slateway had broad, grassy verges on which the cows could graze. And if any farmers whose fields he passed carelessly left their gates open, he took his time in driving his straying cattle back to the road. On the way he had rabbit snares to inspect in the hedges.

Arriving eventually at his own fields, Elisha leaned against a gate and smoked a leisurely pipe before spending half an hour or so cutting hazel rods from his hedges. They would be needed, at some time or another, for wattle hurdles, thatching spars, pea-sticks, faggots or one of the other multitudinous purposes for which villagers employed hazel. Then a stroll back home for a midday meal.

In mid-afternoon he repeated the odyssey, allowing ample time for a yarn with anyone he happened to meet and for setting a few more rabbit snares. The cows went back in their stalls eventually for the afternoon milking, then they were turned into the paddock for the night. Elisha therefore had a bit of time for gardening. Or sometimes he gave a larger farmer a hand with the harvest or haymaking or with the turnip-hoeing – nothing too exacting, mind you; he could please himself what time he knocked off.

Elisha Whitlock was something of an anachronism. He had contrived to perpetuate some seventy years beyond its natural term a way of life that was once commonplace. Under the old dispensation of open fields and commons most of the villagers would have engaged in a similar time-wasting routine. Only then, Elisha's grandfather, whoever he was, would have had common rights, reckoned as the equivalent of an acre, plus three separate acres in different parts of the open fields.

Imagine the comings and goings throughout the long summer days. Cows in twos and threes coming in from the common to be milked, drinking at the ponds and returning to the common for more grazing. Men with scythes or hoes trudging from one field to another. Sheep straying into standing corn as a neglectful shepherd dozed off. Under the eminently fair allocation of fields, Elisha's grandfather, or possibly John Collins, would have one of his acres in the great open field by Bottom Way, another by White Way (on the Salisbury road) and a third at the far end of Slateway. The time used in walking from one to another must have been incalculable, especially as most of the other men in the parish were doing the same and could hardly have passed each other along the stony or grassy tracks without pausing for a word or two. The fields around Pitton must have been alive with people, though how many of them were engaged in productive activity at any one moment is anybody's guess.

Let us try to identify some of these villagers at the beginning of our story, the year 1800. The documentary sources of information are quite considerable, though requiring careful study. They include parish registers of baptisms, marriages and deaths, censuses, parish account books, wills, sales transactions, sundry other legal documents, private letters and so on.

For Pitton, however, we have in addition two important and comprehensive surveys, complete with detailed maps. The first is the Enclosure Award, dated 1810, the second, the Tithe Award Map, prepared when tithe was commuted from a payment in kind to an annual cash payment, in 1838. They serve as a check on each other.

The tithe map, with the accompanying schedule, is a beautiful document, with copperplate writing and meticulously drawn field boundaries and other features. It is, however, interested only in tithe units and so does not record (or only incidentally in a few instances) the actual houses, just the enclosure around each, for which tithe was payable.

The enclosure award map is less clear. Here, too, the compiler is interested chiefly in fields, with their acreage and ownership. Many of the roadside boundaries are marked with blobs, indicating trees or tall hedges, and in some instances it is difficult to decide what is supposed to be a tree and what a building. Although the farms are clearly depicted, less care has been taken with the cottages. No real distinction is made between cottages and farm buildings, and independent evidence reveals that what, on the map, appears to be one cottage was in reality a pair.

With these provisos and the use of a magnifying glass, it is possible to obtain a reasonably accurate picture of the village in 1810. The author's estimate is that Pitton comprised between eighty and a hundred inhabited houses in that year. A surprising number of these were still in existence in the years 1912–39, the period of *The Lost Village*, and some still survive, though the great era of destruction covered the decades 1950–80. Moreover, the author's father, who was born at Pitton in 1874 and lived there all his life, was able to provide a great deal of information on houses that had been demolished in his time or a little earlier.

Another major source of information about nineteenth-century Pitton consists of the decennial censuses, of which one of the best and most informative is that of 1851. The number of houses occupied at that date was ninety-eight, which tallies neatly with the author's estimate of eighty to a hundred in 1819. Nearly all of them can be identified with those referred to in the 1819 award and could also be identified by the author's father.

A major disaster occurred in the year 1863 or 1864, when a fire destroyed two farms, their buildings and several cottages closely packed together in the centre of the village. Allowing for that event, the number of changes in the composition and appearance of the village in the nineteenth century was quite minimal. Apart from the scene of the fire, the village would have been easily recognizable in, say, 1900, to a villager of 1819.

That being so, it is fair to assume that no great changes occurred in the ten years prior to 1810 and that the award map projects a reasonably accurate picture of Pitton at the beginning of the century.

Now, the 1851 census gives a total population of 409 souls, domiciled in ninety-seven houses (there was one uninhabited cottage). That gives an average of about four persons per household. Assuming that there were ninety inhabited houses in Pitton in 1800, the population, in the same ratio, would have been around 360. It may have been rather less, for a general increase in population in England occurred in the first half of the nineteenth century.

Be that as it may, the seventeen families catalogued in the 1810 award would, at four per family, account for sixty-one persons. That would leave around 300, or five-sixths of the village population, unaccounted for. Presumably their holdings on the common and in the

open fields were too small to be considered in the award.
There were too many of them to be categorized as
agricultural labourers at that early date, though that is
what most of them subsequently became. No provision
seems to have been made for them in the enclosure award,
though there is a hint that the field awarded to John
Jennings may have been so allocated for that purpose. The
author's father had a dim recollection that 'Jenningses' or
some field near it was also known as 'Poor Folks', but that
was only hearsay.

With this preamble, let us take a random dip into the
records and see what other information we can unearth
concerning the people of Pitton at the watershed between
the eighteenth and nineteenth centuries.

To start with, here is a paternity case. It is an
impressively drawn legal document, beginning with the
trumpeting words 'Know All Men' and presenting the
deposition of the importunate mother-to-be.

Whereas Jane Hatcher of the parish of Pitton and Farley in the
county of Wilts aforesaid, singlewoman in and by her
voluntary examination taken in writing and upon oath on the
twentyfirst day of this present September hath declared that
she is great with child and that the said child is likely to be
born a Bastard and to become chargeable to the said parish of
Pitton and Farley, And in and by her said Examination hath
charged John White late of the parish of Winterslow in the
county of Wilts, labourer, with begetting the child she now
gooth with and with being the true and only father thereof,
Now the Condition of this Obligation is such that for the
Relief of the said Parish of Pitton and Farley and for the
Maintenance of the said Bastard Child, if the above bounden
John White and Robert White or either of them, their or either
of their Heirs Executors or Administrators Do and Shall well
and truly pay or cause to be paid unto the Churchwardens
and Overseers of the Poor of the said parish of Pitton and
Farley or some or one of them for the Time Being the Sum of
Twenty Shillings to defray the charges of the Lying-in of the
said Jane Hatcher and do and shall also pay or cause to be paid
to the Churchwardens or Overseers of the poor of the parish of
Pitton and Farley for the Time Being or some or one of them
the Sum of One Shilling of lawful Money of Great Britain

weekly and every week for and towards the Support and Maintenance of the said Bastard Child until the said Bastard Child shall attain to the age of Eight years, if the same shall so long live and be chargeable to the said Parish; And also at the end of eight years, to be computed from the time of the Birth of the said Bastard Child ... do and shall well and truly pay or cause to be paid unto the Churchwardens or Overseers of the Poor of the parish of Pitton and Farley aforesaid ... the sum of Two pounds to be applied towards the putting out of the same Bastard Child to be an Apprentice, then this Obligation to be void, but if it shall happen that this said sum of Twenty shillings shall be behind and unpaid or the said Sum of One Shilling shall not be paid weekly and every Week when and as often as the same ought to have been paid or if default shall be made in payment of the said Sum of Two pounds in the manner or for the use abovementioned, Then this Bond or Obligation to stand and remain in full Force.

Sealed and Delivered / being first duly stampt / in the presence of ... [two gentlemen whose signatures are not decipherable].

And the document is completed by the 'Marks' of John White and Robert White – scrawled crosses, for neither of them could write. One assumes that Robert was probably the father of the hot-blooded young miscreant John.

For purposes of comparison, farm wages would then have been about 7 shillings a week; the price of beef and mutton, 4 pence per pound, and of cheese 4½ pence. So John and Robert were accepting a fairly formidable obligation. Perhaps it is permissible to imagine a smirk of satisfaction on the faces of the compilers of the agreement, implying, 'Now wriggle out of that if you can!' And our sympathies are bound to be with the poor Bastard Child, due to be bound as an apprentice at the age of eight if it should live that long – a matter about which, it was recognized, there would be some doubt.

We do not know what happened to Jane Hatcher's child, but records demonstrate that such transactions between parishes were common in the late eighteenth and early nineteenth centuries.

To give another example, there is an order for the removal of William Shergold from the parish of East Dean (about six miles distant) to the parish of Pitton and Farley in 1843. It is signed by a justice of the peace and states that, unless the overseers of the poor of Pitton appeal within twenty-one days, William Shergold will be removed and conveyed to Pitton. Further clauses of the order reveal that William Shergold is 'the illegitimate child of Charlotte Viveash, deceased' and is 'now aged about four years'. This episode evidently had a happy outcome. The original order was dated 29 May, and on 25 June another rescinded it. The overseers of the poor of East Dean 'consent and agree to abandon the Order'. In the parlance of a similar agreement, they accept William as 'an inhabitant legally settled in their parish'. Presumably some of his relations agreed to be responsible for him.

A much more complex case occurred in 1799. It requires a little explanation which can be provided by a document of 1797. This gives notice to Edward Reed, labourer, of Pitton and Farley, that 'he is chosen by ballot and appointed to serve in the Supplementary Militia of the said County of Wilts.' He is required to appear, ten days later, to take the oath and begin his service at the Antelope Inn, Salisbury, unless he shall ' … otherwise produce, for a substitute, a man of the same county, able and fit for service, who shall be approved by the Deputy Lieutenants'. The period of service is 'during the present War and for the Space of one Calendar Month after the end thereof'. If Edward Reed answered the summons, he had a long army service ahead of him, for the war with the French under Napoleon did not end until 1815.

Whether the 1799 document applies to him or not we cannot say. It may do. It is issued by a justice of the peace and concerns one Stephen Foyle, who ' … is a Substitute serving in the Supplementary Militia of the said County of Wilts and is now in actual Service'. But it now appears that Stephen Foyle ' … hath left Mary his wife and two Children, both under ten years of age now dwelling in the Parish of Britford and unable to support themselves'. So, under an Act of Parliament, the magistrate now makes an order for the churchwardens and overseers of the poor of the parish of Pitton and Farley to repay to the overseers of the poor of the parish of Britford the sum of 3s. 9d. weekly for the maintenance of Mary Foyle and her children for as long as Stephen is serving in the militia!

One can visualize the scenario. Edward Reed, labourer, or whoever was chosen by ballot, is aghast at the prospect of leaving home and going to war for an indefinite period. In Salisbury next market day he advertises his predicament in one of the city pubs. No doubt much advice is proffered, and by some means Stephen Foyle is produced. He is willing to be persuaded, doubtless with some financial inducements, to act as substitute. Probably there were other factors in the case, unknown to us. Stephen may have been in trouble already. Maybe he was unemployed and did not know which way to turn. Perhaps he was a born wanderer who was tired of being married to Mary. Anyway, the bargain was struck, Stephen was accepted for the militia, and Edward was free to remain at home, working on the farm.

It seems more than likely that the plight of Mary Foyle and her two children did not become known, either to the churchwardens of Britford or to those of Pitton and Farley, until later. When it did, the Britford people quite rightly called upon Pitton and Farley to support her. Poor Edward Reed, who until then was doubtless congratulating himself on his escape from military service, must have been highly unpopular in his home village when the news broke. There is no record of his having to make any contribution to the fund.

The system of parish responsibility for its poor dates from the year 1601, when, under an Act of Queen Elizabeth I, the state acknowledged its duty for the relief of the indigent poor, which, before the Reformation, had been undertaken by the Church. Parishes were required to levy a poor rate for the purpose, the collection and administration of the rate being entrusted to local overseers appointed by justices of the peace. By later enactments these overseers could delegate their duties to paid guardians.

The overseers, or the guardians acting for them, had the option of granting either indoor or outdoor relief. Until 1722 most relief consisted of a cash payment to those in need, but an Act of Parliament in that year gave an impetus to the construction of parish workhouses. These became useful dustbins for the dumping of the inconvenient parasites of the community. There is no record of one at Pitton, but Farley is known to have had a workhouse down Penny's Lane.

A cross-section of parish workhouse inmates is given by the poet George Crabbe, writing in the last decades of the eighteenth century:

Their is yon House that holds the Parish Poor,
Whose walls of mud scarce bear the broken door;
There, where the putrid vapours, flagging, play,
And the dull wheel hums doleful through the day;
There Children dwell who know no Parents' care;
Parents, who know no Children's love, dwell there!
Heart-broken Matrons on their joyless bed,
Forsaken Wives and Mothers never wed;
Dejected Widows with unheeded tears,
And crippled Age, with more than childhood fears;
The Lame, the Blind, and, far the happiest they!
The moping Idiot and the Madman gay.
Here too the Sick their final doom receive,
Here brought, amid the scenes of grief, to grieve ...

The parish workhouse was, however, for those who could not work. Able-bodied men and women were required to earn their keep. Several alternative systems existed at the beginning of the nineteenth century. The guardians might employ the paupers on work for the parish, or they could share out the paupers among the local employers (mainly, of course, farmers), the employer paying what he felt he was able. The guardians kept this money, passing to the labourer just sufficient for the maintenance of himself and his family, but making up any deficit from the rates.

The motives of the 'churchwardens and overseers of the poor' in the sample documents given above are thus abundantly clear. Each parish is eager to get rid of any person liable to be a dependent pauper. The authorities at Pitton and Farley were neatly caught out by Stephen Foyle of Britford but in general they seem to have been pretty vigilant.

In Elizabethan times 'sturdy beggars' became a national

nuisance, the Reformation having destroyed their traditional source of relief while the growth of sheep-farming tended to make whole villages redundant. As the nursery rhyme, written about that time, chants:

> Hark! hark! the dogs do bark!
> The beggars are coming to town!
> Some in rags, and some in jags,
> And some in a velvet gown.

The problems created by these wandering mobs became so serious that ferocious measures had to be taken to deter them. Any vagrant appearing without any visible means of support in a village was liable to be conducted to the parish boundary, stripped to the waist at the tail of a cart and whipped soundly all the way. Often the penalty was applied indiscriminately, even to a lonely, abandoned woman trying to find her way back to her birthplace.

By the end of the eighteenth century more humane attitudes had prevailed, as is illustrated by the following extract from Salisbury's Quarter Sessions Rolls. It happens to refer not to Pitton or Farley but to next-door Winterslow. Note that the parish official in this instance is called 'the Tythingman'.

In February 1791 six vagrants were suffocated in their lodging-room at East Winterslow by someone carelessly setting fire to the straw of their beds. There is no account of the incident in the Quarter Sessions Rolls of that year, but in 1793, at the Sessions held at New Sarum on 9th April, the Tythingman of East Winterslow presented the following bill for payment:–

Bill of the Tything-man of East Winterslow of extraordinary Expences on Accot of Six Vagrants who were suffocated by accident.

	£. s. d.
1791.	
Feb.10th. Doctor Bloxham's bill for attendance on and medicine for two paupers	1. 5. 0
Mr.Williams' bill for six shrouds	0.17. 9
Jacob Burden's bill for six coffins	2. 2. 0
Mr. Fiander's bill for burying six vagrants	0.15. 0
Paid the Jurymen	0.16. 0

Paid two women for laying out six vagrants	0. 8. 0
The Tythingman's Extra trouble on acct of the said six persons	1. 1. 0
	£7. 4. 9

The account was examined and allowed.

Rather more detail is given in the *Salisbury and Winchester Journal* for 14 February 1791:

A most horrid catastrophe happened last Wednesday at Winterslow, near this city. In an outbuilding, belonging to Farmer Hayden, were lodged three men, a woman and two children, who had been brought thither that day in a pass cart, on their way to their respective parishes in the West, and having been comfortably refreshed and indulged with a fire, which they promised to put out, they were left to their repose about nine o'clock in the evening. Early the next morning it was discovered that the premises had by some accident taken fire, and that the woman, her two children and one of the men were burnt to death, and the other two miserable wretches so dreadfully scorched that, notwithstanding every possible professional assistance was immediately administered by Mr. Bloxham, surgeon, of Stockbridge, they survived but a short time. Mr. Forsyth, the coroner, took inquests on their several bodies – verdicts, suffocated and scorched to death.

It is interesting to note that here everything had been legally arranged. Wherever the travellers came from, someone (maybe themselves) had provided sufficient funds for the journey. They were supplied with a 'pass cart', to save them from walking, and evidently on arrival had presented themselves to the Tythingman, who was sufficiently impressed by their credentials to provide them with a meal and a fire.

Earlier it seems that in some parishes the officials were so anxious to be rid of uninvited visitors that they were prepared to pay them to move on. In the churchwarden's accounts for Pitton and Farley for the year 1722 John Whitlock, retiring churchwarden, includes two separate items 'Paid to Travellers' – one for 1s.3d. and one for one shilling.

Incidentally, for Pitton and Farley the rates accounts

seem to have been kept separately. They do not appear in the churchwardens' accounts, where the most regularly occurring items are for 'visitation expenses' (by the bishop), bread and wine, and the churchwardens' expenses for preparing the accounts. Also fairly regular are amounts paid for vermin-control – a fox's head (one shilling) and forty-one dozen sparrow heads (6s.10d.) in 1722; twenty-one dozen sparrows at 6 pence a dozen, and fifty-five dozen sparrows at 3 pence a dozen, together with twenty-three hedgehogs at 4 pence each in 1830. Poor hedgehogs, and poor sparrows! In all probability the latter included many other small birds than house-sparrows – greenfinches, chaffinches and hedge-sparrows, for instance.

Milking

4   The Threatening Storm

The dramatic changes that exploded in Pitton and Farley in the second decade of the nineteenth century and revolutionized the traditional way of life had their origins a hundred years earlier. Their inception was political.

In the reigns of the later Stuarts, from Charles II to Anne, political power became polarized on two major parties, namely the Tories, who were the party of High Anglican landowners, and the Whigs, dominated by dissenting merchants and financiers. The Tories were in the ascendant during the last years of Queen Anne's reign. They would gladly have welcomed her half-brother James as her successor if only he had consented to become a Protestant, but this he refused to do. So on the death of Anne the throne passed to the next Protestant heir, the German head of the House of Hanover. The new king, George I, who spoke not a word of English and who was much more interested in Hanover than in Britain, naturally left the managements of affairs to his ministers.

Because the Tories had been intriguing to prevent George's accession, the first administration of the new reign was Whig. Thereafter the Whigs played their cards so astutely for the next forty-five years (from 1714 to 1761) they kept the Tories out of office. Sulking and resentful, the Tory landowners retired to their country estates,

forming Jacobite clubs at which they toasted 'the king over
the water'. They had a chance to translate words into
action in 1715, the first year of George's reign, but it came
too early. They were not organized for a successful
rebellion, and the rising in support of the Old Pretender
was confined to Scotland and a few of the northern
counties and was suppressed without difficulty.

The challenge presented by the Young Pretender,
Bonnie Prince Charlie, thirty years later was altogether
more formidable. At the head of a Scottish army, the
glamorous young prince marched south as far as Derby, at
a moment when the greater part of England's small army
was engaged in the Netherlands, fighting against the
French. All that was needed was a rising of the Tory
landowners, still professing Jacobite sentiments, and the
Stuarts would have had a good chance of being back on
the throne. It didn't happen. For the past thirty years the
Tory landowners, excluded from political power, had been
concentrating their considerable talents on improving
their country estates. They had become thoroughly
interested in their achievements and were full of plans of
what to do next. When the challenge came, they found
they were unwilling to risk everything on the hazards of a
civil war. So the opportunity slipped away.

The Tories had to wait a further sixteen years before
they could assume what they held to be their rightful
place in the control of affairs of state. By then there was a
new king, no foreigner but English born and bred and,
moreover, one who, like them, took a pride in his
extensive country estates. After a few disastrous experiences in politics, George III was content to leave national
affairs to his ministers. His aspirations were, above all else,
to be an English country gentleman.

What had the Tory landowners been up to in their long
exile? Apart from building new mansions, creating new
parks and enjoying an elaborate social life, they had
become interested in agricultural improvements. Two new
crops, clover and turnips, had been introduced from the
Netherlands, and the old English three-course rotation
had to be adapted to fit them in.

Two new concepts had to be digested. One went by the

name of 'Up-and-Down Husbandry', which later generations of farmers knew as 'alternate husbandry' or 'ley
farming'. It is a system under which each field is devoted
to a period of years under grass followed by a period of
years of arable cropping. The other neatly dovetails this
programme into a four-course rotation, of which there
were a number of versions. One of the most popular was
the Norfolk four-course rotation, pioneered by Viscount
Townshend on his estates in Norfolk, who from his
enthusiasm for the turnip crop became known as 'Turnip
Townshend'. The programme consists of: first year,
turnips; second year, barley; third year, grass and clover
(from sown seeds); fourth year, wheat. It required both
the turnips and the grass and clover crops to be grazed by
penned sheep. It naturally resulted in vastly improved
crops of wheat and barley.

To fit such a programme into the old open-field system
was very difficult indeed. It was not impossible, but
success required the co-operation of a whole community
of villagers. One obdurate diehard could wreck a
promising scheme.

Enclosures were not, of course, an invention of the
eighteenth century. They had been going on almost from
time immemorial. A typical though very minor example of
an enclosure is given in *The Lost Village*. Morris Baugh, the
village thatcher in the late nineteenth and early twentieth
century, lived in a thatched cottage on one edge of what
survived of the village green. On the green itself, on the
far side of the track from his cottage garden, he dumped a
substantial heap of faggots and bundles of spar-gads. No
one objected, so after a time he erected a rail fence, to keep
passing cows from 'hooking them about'. The area thus
enclosed was gradually extended. Nobody objected and,
before he died, it was tacitly assumed to be the property of
Mr Baugh.

It was a process which had been going on for centuries.
Sometimes the encroacher was a villager or peasant, like
Mr Baugh; sometimes a squatter seeking a site for a house;
sometimes the lord of the manor. The criterion was simply
whether he could get away with it, and naturally the lord
of the manor had the best chance.

In most instances, the encroachment was made on common land. Tampering with the open fields was a much more delicate matter, though some schemes went through by general consent. They needed general agreement by everyone concerned and had to be registered with the Court of Chancery. However, as the landowners of the early eighteenth century came to realize, the key role of enclosures in their plans for the improvements of their estates, they also came to recognize the potentialities of private Acts of Parliament. They worked out the procedure to a nicety. To set the ball rolling it needed only one owner of land in a manor to petition for an enclosure. Until 1774 he could do so without giving any notice to his neighbours, and there were instances of the arrival of officials to apportion the land being the first intimation to the rest of the parish of what was afoot. After 1774 a notice of his intentions had to be nailed to the church door for three Sundays in August or September.

The petition presented to Parliament was required to set out reasons for the proposed enclosure, describing the faults of the existing system and enlarging on the benefits of the new one. Thomas Davis of Longleat, reporting to the Board of Agriculture in the early years of the eighteenth century, gives an objective account of how enclosures worked out for villagers on the chalklands of Wiltshire:

> A farmer worth £200 a year will, perhaps, in consequence of having his land in larger units, [he writes], be able to reduce his number of horses one-third; he will have it in his power to sow clover, sainfoin, etc., for hay and to raise turnips and rape for winter food for his sheep; and consequently he will not only increase his flock but he will also winter them at home. Although by this mode of husbandry he must necessarily reduce the number of acres of corn, yet he will be able, by his additional number of sheep, to manure his land much better, and he will probably raise more grain than he did before.

Davis was well aware, however, that the smaller farmers were bound to suffer:

> A man with land worth £40 a year [he admits] will certainly have the conveniency of having his land brought together in fewer pieces. But as it seldom happens that he could plough

his land with fewer than three horses before such a division, neither can he now do with less. He has now no enclosed pasture to put these horses in nor common to turn them on. His right on the Downs being too small to make it worth his while to take an allotment for a sheep down (of perhaps twenty acres, two miles from home) he takes an increase to his arable land, in the fields near home, in lieu of it. But now he can keep no sheep on this allotment, nor would it be worth his while to employ a shepherd for so few, even if he could. Without sheep he is driven to some expensive manure to dung his land, because, having so little pasture land and no cow commons, he can keep no cows to make dung with his straw ...

Davis acknowledges the argument that such farms are too small to be economic. No one, starting afresh, would consider it prudent to create such small units. 'But men of this description are already here,' he points out. 'They are settled on the spot. It is, in many instances, their own. Justice will not let them be dispossessed without their consent; policy and humanity forbid that they should be injured, even with their consent.'

Davis's sentiments do him credit, but he must have been wearing rose-tinted spectacles to avoid seeing what was going on all around him. When a petition for enclosure was presented to Parliament and accepted, permission was given for the necessary Bill to be introduced. This Bill was given its first and second readings and then passed to a committee which would, at least in theory, duly consider any objections and then report back to Parliament. The Bill would be passed, sent to the House of Lords for approval and finally receive the royal assent. This key committee was entrusted to a single Member of Parliament who could load it with as many other members as he chose. On the principle 'You scratch my back and I'll scratch yours', the committees served the interests of their friends in Parliament and made scant regard to the protests of peasants in distant fields.

Nevertheless, the provisions of an Enclosure Act seem fair enough on paper. A typical Act states:

The open common fields, commons, marshes, etc., were to be divided among the several persons according to their respective Rights and Interests, due regard being paid to

Quality, Quantity and Situation, and the allotments being placed as near the Homesteads, etc., as is consistent with general convenience.

All houses erected twenty years or more before the Act, and the sites of all such houses, to be considered as ancient messuages entitled to right of common, with the exception of houses built on encroachments, the owners of which are to have whatever allotment the Commissioners think fair and reasonable.

The poor were taken care of by retaining an area of common land for communal use, as in times past. If thought advisable, the trustees (normally the vestry meeting of the parish) could enclose part of it and let it to a farmer, using the rent for the benefit of the poor. Many villages, among them Pitton (as we shall see later), still have plots of land, now fields, bearing the name 'Poor Folks' or 'Poor Patch'. They seem to have been enclosed and rented off without any attempt at commonage and are usually in a remote corner of the parish.

Getting a private member's Bill through Parliament was naturally an expensive business. The lawyers and, at a later stage, the commissioners had to be paid, and doubtless there was a great deal of surreptitious bribery. All these expenses had to be borne by the estate, so usually a section of common land was set aside to meet them. Who would buy such land? Why, the principal landowners. It has been estimated that £3 an acre was probably about the average a man would have to pay for his title to land acquired under an Enclosure Act, and he was allowed to mortgage the land to raise the cash, if he could find an investor. Major landowners and the larger farmers might have little difficulty in raising the loan, but for cottagers and the small farmers, often illiterate, the transaction was impossible. There are instances of their selling their allotments to their wealthier neighbours simply in order to pay the legal expenses.

As for the motives behind the enclosures, in spite of the pious expressions of sentiments about the improvement of agriculture, some petitions to Parliament were initiated for altogether baser reasons. Surviving correspondence and other records reveal that many of the gentry involved in enclosures were enmeshed in a web of debts, from which the acquisition of more land by way of an Enclosure Act offered the only way out.

Once, too, the owning of a great country estate had become fashionable, there was a rush to join in. Everyone wanted to outdo his neighbour. This was the age of 'Capability' Brown, the great landscape artist who tended to regard the rural scene as a bare canvas on which he could create his masterpieces. His nickname came from his habit, when called in to advise, of cocking his head and observing, 'Yes, I see great capability of improvement here.'

The nucleus of the country estate was, of course, the 'big house', which had a parallel in the villa of late Roman times. Many country mansions assumed the proportions and grandeur of palaces. Blenheim Palace (Oxfordshire), Ashridge Park (Hertfordshire), Wentworth Woodhouse (Yorkshire) and Raynham Hall (Norfolk) are outstanding examples, but every English county has its quota, still dominating the rural scene. Their interiors, equally imposing, were exquisitely designed and furnished and were replete with art treasures.

The immediate setting of a great house comprised gardens and a park. When early country mansions began to replace the great abbeys after the Reformation, formality was the current fashion. A typical design shows a series of rectangular plots on either side of a broad central avenue leading in a dead straight line to the exact centre of the house. The trees, the pools, the flowerbeds, the pergolas are all arranged with mathematical precision. Gardeners of that age were skilful in pruning trees to throw out branches at the correct height and angle to transform an avenue into a symmetrically arched cloister.

Later the vogue switched to curves and circles, and a better appreciation of sylvan surroundings developed. Guests at country houses were invited to walk round the grounds after lunch, and their leisurely perambulations would frequently be enlivened by the discovery or new and unheralded delights. At Wardour, Wiltshire, Lord Arundell realized that he possessed an enviable treasure in his ruined castle, which had been spectacularly damaged during the Civil War. From his new castle on the other side of his lake he used to take his guests across the park and regale them with a lively account of its history. Often on summer afternoons they took a picnic, which they ate sitting on the lawns by the lake.

This imaginative nobleman conceived a brilliant idea for a further 'improvement'. He decided that the hillside behind the ruin was the ideal site for a grotto, then a fashionable feature of a great estate. The materials for it were conveniently available on one of his farms, only a mile or so away. They consisted of a group of immense sarsen stones arranged in a circle, very similar to Stonehenge – or, perhaps more precisely, to Avebury – and evidently belonging to the same prehistoric millennium. There were dozens of them. Lord Arundell assembled an army of men, horses and wagons and carted them all over to Old Wardour, where the visitor may still see them, built into a series of caves and grottoes. Human bones unearthed under the centre of the circle are said to have been reinterred under a group of three of the stones at their new site.

Not far away, at Stourhead, once the home of the Colt Hoare family but now National Trust property, the owners had no such asset ready to hand and so had to rely on their ingenuity. A stroll by the lake there, by paths that lead over lawns and through clearings amid stands of majestic trees, offers a succession of vistas of which the focal point is either a Palladian summerhouse or, on the far side of the lake, Stourhead House itself. The summerhouse was an important feature of the estate in the days of its glory, for here, as they rested from the exertions which had brought them thus far, the guests partook of afternoon tea – a platoon of servants having preceded them. By some means or another, however, the Colt Hoares did manage to acquire the Bristol Cross, which stood in the centre of Bristol for 400 years from 1373 and is now a central feature of the gardens.

A less amiable characteristic of the rural estate-owners was their obsession with game preservation. From time immemorial, game laws have been a fertile source of friction. Deer were the wild creatures to which the earliest were applied, and the savagery of William the Conqueror's forest laws is notorious. At least the Norman kings, and their Saxon predecessors, could claim that poachers were not only interfering with the king's sport, they were helping themselves to the royal dinner.

In the century before our story begins, two new factors became important. One was the development of efficient sporting guns; the other, an accelerating increase in population. Between 1702, when Queen Anne came to the throne, and 1801 the population of England and Wales rose from 5½ million to nearly 11 million. And as during that period the population was still predominantly rural, it is evident that the countryside was becoming overcrowded. The wastes of forests, heath and fen in which medieval villages hid like sequestered islands were fast disappearing, and with them their wild denizens. Except in certain well-forested regions, such as Cranborne Chase in Dorset, deer were soon too scarce to afford regular sport to gentlemen. Simultaneously the improvements in sporting guns, allowing birds to be shot flying, began to decimate partridges. The attention of estate-owners turned to pheasants.

Pheasants, however, are not native to Britain. They are thought to have been brought into the country in Roman times and perhaps reintroduced in the Middle Ages, but, susceptible to the chills of the English climate and vulnerable to predators, they could by no means sustain the artillery onslaught now launched upon them. Their numbers had to be reinforced and some protection afforded them. In 1787 the Duke of Marlborough started to hatch pheasants' eggs under broody hens on his estate at Blenheim, and his example was soon widely followed. The cult of the pheasant had arrived.

Back in 1723 Parliament had passed what became known as 'the Black Act', which introduced fifty new capital offences to the statute book. Directed largely against deer-poachers, it was supposed to have been an emergency measure for three years only but was still in operation in the first few decades of the nineteenth century. A man could be hanged not only for killing a deer but for being in possession of venison illegally obtained, for being found with a blackened face on a game preserve, for sending anonymous threatening letters, for cutting down trees on a private estate and even for harbouring a person suspected of these as well as a whole host of associated offences. The ultimate penalty was now being exacted from the countryman with the temerity to kill a pheasant.

Logically, the owner of a pheasant-rearing preserve had some justification for his attitude. His pheasants cost him a lot of money. He needed to employ an increasing army of keepers, both for rearing his birds and for protecting them against poachers. On the perimeter and in strategic positions within his estate he had planted shelter belts and coverts, often of alien conifers, which transformed the face of the countryside. He expected to be allowed to pursue his chosen sport in peace.

His less affluent neighbours had other ideas. Much of the land he claimed they considered theirs by right, it having been former common land. And on the common land they had been accustomed to regard the local fauna as legitimate game, for anyone who could take it. There was little scope for compromise.

A poaching war which took shape in the eighteenth century was pursued with increasing bitterness. Pitched battles were fought between keepers and poachers, in which there are fatal casualties on both sides. In the early years of the nineteenth century spring-guns and man-traps were introduced. Spring-guns proving not very reliable, being responsible for numerous accidents to innocent persons and keepers, had a relatively short career, but the man-trap was a feature of rural life on some estates for much of the nineteenth century. Richard Jefferies, the Wiltshire naturalist writing in the 1870s and 1880s, found that many of his informants were thoroughly familiar with it. They called it 'the Iron Wolf'.

Clearing the Ground.

5 The Coming of the Hedges

We return now to the three horsemen of the episode that forms our first chapter. Both Lord Wilmot and Stephen Fox escaped across the Channel with their king and remained loyal to him throughout his years of exile. Stephen, whose great asset was evidently his mathematical ability, acted as steward to the King through that period of severe financial stringency. Somehow he contrived to stretch the slender royal resources farther than seemed reasonably possible.

After the Restoration he was rewarded with the post of Paymaster General to the Forces. Critics have commented that among the first persons he took care to pay was himself, but that is perhaps unfair. He behaved as was expected of a public official in that age, and a contemporary, in an epitaph, recorded that Sir Stephen (he had been duly knighted) '... was worth at least £200,000, honestly gotten and unenvied, which is next to a miracle'!

Settled at the Court of Charles II, Sir Stephen married Elizabeth Whittle, daughter of a Lancashire gentleman. They had six sons and three daughters, and of the sons only one, Charles, survived. Having accumulated all that money, Sir Stephen was ambitious to establish a distinguished dynasty but was deeply disappointed in his surviving son, who seemed to be doing nothing about starting a family.

So, after the death of his first wife, in 1696, the old man (he was then nearly eighty) decided to redeem the situation. He courted and proposed marriage to a somewhat surprised Margaret (or Christian) Hope, daughter of a Lincolnshire clergyman. As Sir Richard Colt Hoare, the contemporary historian of Wiltshire, delicately summarized the situation:

> Being now advanced nearly to the age of fourscore years, and perceiving no likelihood that his only son Charles should have issue, and unwilling that so plentiful an estate should go out of the name ... he began to entertain thoughts of marrying (for he was of a vegete and hale constitution) and had spent his life with much temperance and regularity, that he did not, without reason, promise himself very happy effects from second nuptials. He therefore fixed upon a young gentlewoman, Mrs. Margaret Hope, daughter of a clergyman of that name, at Grantham in Lincolnshire, and made her the honourable offer of his person and fortune, which the lady, who at first took it for a piece of gallantry, was too discreet not to accept. This nuptial was blessed by the birth of twins, in gratitude for which he fixed his eye on the impropriation of Shepton Montague, in Somerset ...
> By his second marriage he had two sons, 1. Stephen, b. 1706 (Earl of Ilchester) and 2. Henry (Earl of Holland).

As a matter of fact, Sir Richard did not get his facts quite straight.

Sir Stephen Fox died, a contented old man, in 1716. His long life was crowned with greater success than falls to the lot of most, and his final ambition looked set to be fulfilled. His unsatisfactory eldest son by his first marriage predeceased him, dying in 1703, but now there were two more little boys to carry on the illustrious family he hoped he had founded. For Margaret (alias Christian) did all that could have been expected of her. She gave her husband a daughter, Charlotte, in 1703, a son Stephen in 1704, and twins, Henry and Christian (a girl) in 1707.

In fact, the boys did even better than he could have anticipated. Thirty years after Sir Stephen's death Stephen was created the first Earl of Ilchester and Henry the first

Earl of Holland. The following generations attained even loftier heights. Lord Holland's third son was the great statesman Charles James Fox, who so strongly opposed Lord North's administration which lost Britain the United States of America. He was equally formidable in his opposition to William Pitt and the war with Napoleon. His work was carried on by his nephew, another Henry Fox, who was the third Lord Holland and had a distinguished parliamentary career, being for a time Lord Privy Seal.

Old Sir Stephen always maintained his links with his birthplace. Towards the end of his life he gave to Farley a new church and also built and endowed an attractive row of almshouses (Fox's Hospital) which are still one of the treasures of the village. All Saints' Church seems such a typical Wren church that it has often been so described, a theory which has gained credence from the knowledge that Sir Stephen and Sir Christopher Wren were friends. The architect was, in fact, Alexander Fort, who had worked with Wren at Kensington Palace and Hampton Court. Both Sir Stephen and his wife were buried in the new church.

The dynasty Sir Stephen had in mind was to be one of rural landowners, like most of their contemporaries of the same class, and his sons, the Earls of Ilchester and Holland, fulfilled that ambition for him. What was more natural than that they should seek their estates in their native soil? At some time fairly early in the eighteenth century the Earl of Ilchester acquired the manor of Pitton and Farley, though as a lessee, it seems, for according to the Enclosure Act, which received the royal assent in 1810, the lords of the manor then were 'the Dean and Chapter of the Cathedral Church of the blessed Virgin Mary of Sarum'. The family also owned at least one farm in the neighbouring parish of West Grimstead.

At around 1767 Sir Stephen's grandson, the second Earl of Holland, bought the manor of West Winterslow from a Revd Dr Thistlethwayte, descendant of a Yorkshire family who had bought the property at the time of the Reformation and had lived there ever since. (Incidentally, one wonders how the Wiltshire villagers contrived to twist their tongues around an alien name like Thistlethwayte!

Remembering how old men in his youth used to refer to thistles as 'dheesles', the author suggests that they probably said 'Dheestledwait' or something of the sort.)

Perhaps because he was unable to buy the Pitton and Farley property outright, the Earl of Ilchester was an absentee landlord, living on another country estate at Melbury, in Dorset. He tended to value the Pitton and Farley land chiefly for the revenue derived from the rents and for the sporting rights, which he travelled up to enjoy several times during autumn and winter.

The Earl of Holland, however, determined to make Winterslow his country seat and to that end set about building a splendid and fashionable mansion. Twice the work was interrupted by fire, the second occurring while a ball to celebrate the completion of the building was in progress. Discouraged, the Holland family decided to cut their losses at Winterslow and transferred their resources to another estate they owned nearer London. It served their descendants well, for although the Holland House they built there was then in open country, the estate around it now comprises Mayfair and much of the West End of London.

Little remains at Winterslow of the regime of the Hollands. The house they built stood in a large meadow in the centre of West Winterslow, known to the more senior inhabitants of the village as 'the Pleasure Ground'. Prominent features in it are several venerable cedars; an old man, Whitmarsh, said in perhaps the 1850s that he remembered helping young Lady Mary Fox to plant them before the fire. On three sides the field, which was once evidently the home park, is bounded by a shelter belt of mature beeches, doubtless planted about the same time. Even more enduring, being likely to survive long after the trees have gone, are certain place-names, clearly borrowed from the Hollands' London estate. Thus Winterslow has a Soho and a Pimlico, while Pitton possesses a Piccadilly.

Local tradition has it that when the third Earl of Holland inherited the title and came to live at Winterslow, he brought with him three families of retainers from Switzerland. These were the Le Roys, Hatchetts and Annetts, who have been prominent in the life of the village, and indeed of the Salisbury district, ever since. The earliest Le Roy, the earl's steward, changed his name to King, the French pronunciation of Le Roy being a bit beyond the capacity of most of his new neighbours.

It is possible, too, that Winterslow's celebrated industry of truffle-hunting (of which more later) has a similar origin. Local tradition, set down in the scrapbook of the Winterslow Women's Institute in the 1950s, relates that it originated '250 years ago when a man brought a pack of specially trained poodles from Spain'. Alfred Collins, the last of the truffle-hunters, stated, 'He made his home for the season with people ... close to Stonehenge, leaving the dogs with them during spring and summer and returning to Spain. Eventually he ceased coming and the dogs, increased in number, were sold by the old couple. That is how the industry was taken up by my ancestors.'

It may have been so, though another tradition says that the dogs came to England via one of the ships wrecked off the Irish coast from the Spanish Armada. The Swiss origin sounds just as likely.

Throughout the second half of the eighteenth century the tide of enclosures rolled on inexorably. To begin with, the process was closely linked with the fortunes of the Tory party, but as it became fashionable the Whigs soon joined in. One could not judge from his behaviour in this matter whether a landowner was Whig or Tory.

Between 1702 and 1762 246 private Enclosure Acts, involving some 400,000 acres, were passed by Parliament. With the return of the Tories to power, the flow became a flood. In the next forty years, from 1761 to 1801, no fewer than 2,000 Acts, involving more than 3 million acres, found their way onto the statute book. And from 1802 to 1844 nearly another 2,000 Acts legitimized the enclosure of a further 2,500,000 acres. The torrent culminated in a General Enclosure Act in 1845.

The Enclosure Act for Pitton and Farley came relatively late. A copy in the author's possession records that it received the royal assent on 2 June 1810, in the fiftieth year of King George III. It runs to twenty foolscap pages and comprises 121 clauses, all set out in abstruse legal jargon.

For example, a typical sentence, running through seventeen clauses, consists of 1,152 words without a full-stop!

This is the document which the law required to be nailed to the church porch in the parish concerned (in this instance, the porches of two churches), so that all the parishioners could read it and know what was going on. For many of them it would have been the first intimation that Doomsday was at hand. The fact that most of them were illiterate seemed irrelevant to the authorities. The law had been complied with, and in theory it was fair and correct.

It is helpful to enquire who benefited by the transaction.

The first entity mentioned is 'the Dean and Chapter of the Cathedral Church of the blessed Virgin Mary of Sarum', who are lords of the manor. Doubtless the cathedral clergy regarded their Pitton and Farley property as an investment; there is no evidence that they were actively interested in or engaged in parish affairs. Any benefit accruing to them would be in the form of increased rents, due to the more efficient management of the land.

Next comes 'The Right Honourable Henry Stephen, Earl of Ilchester', who is the lessee of all the land concerned. Now, as an absentee landlord, some of the motives which weighed heavily with those of his contemporaries who were enclosing land outside their back door did not apply to him. He had no interest in creating a compact estate with all the fashionable amenities around a big house. His interest would seem, superficially, to be identical with that of the cathedral, namely the increase in rents due to more efficient farming. However, it is worth bearing in mind that he regarded the parish as a sporting estate, to which all that has been said about the vogue of the pheasant applied. Throughout the century the notes by the local agent of the visits of successive earls are concerned primarily with the game bags. Provision for the protection of game was written into all tenancy agreements, and farmers practising at the end of the century testified that to kill a hare was more than their tenancy was worth.

Topographically, too, the Foxes had distanced themselves from Wiltshire. Their links with their kinsmen in

Pitton from the hill looking west, *c.* 1900

Aerial view of modern Pitton

Ellen, wife of Noah Whitlock, outside the door of the cottage by White Hill where she reared her family. The cottage has long since been demolished

Willow Cottage, in its original state of disrepair

Church Farm, Pitton. Figures are Joshua White and his wife
Julia – the author's grandparents. Snowdrops planted by Julia
in the orchard still bloom every spring

Bowers Farm, Pitton. The farmhouse on the left and the farm
cottage on the right were demolished in the 1960s

Right: Pitton, *c.* 1885. This is a photo of a water-colour painted by a Mr Parsons who was a Pitton resident until shortly after that date when he moved to Durham

Bottom left: Manor Farm, Pitton. A fine Georgian farmhouse demolished by Wiltshire County Council in the late 1960s

Bottom right: Webb's Farm, Pitton. The home of the author for seventeen years, and in Victorian times the home of the Webb family. In the front garden (on the left of the picture) stood a smithy, operated by Moses Webb in the early nineteenth century who made the weather-vane on the spire of Pitton Church. Concealed in the house was what appears to have been a priest's hiding-chamber

Pitton Band in about 1895. Taken at Manor Farm, Pitton. The
two central figures (*seated*) are Charles and Edwin Whitlock

Old photograph of the Pheasant at Winterslow Hutt

Eight Victorian villagers who lived on into the early years of our century.
Front row (l. to r.): Noah White, Uriah Whitlock, Stephen Judd, George Noyce.
Back row: Noah Whitlock, Stephen Seaward, Alfred Legge, Arthur Whitlock

Group of Pitton and Farley veterans at Devizes early in the 1900s. The photograph shows a muster of all the older inhabitants of the villages to oppose a closure of footpaths through the Clarendon Estate, which the villagers claimed had been open from time immemorial. Most of the characters cannot now be identified, but the last on the right is Arthur Whitlock

Old cottages by White Hill, Pitton

Ruins of the cottages pictured above. Taken soon after their
destruction by fire (caused by a spark from a passing threshing-
machine engine igniting the thatched roof)

Farley and Pitton had become tenuous. The Selwyn letters, dealing with the year 1775, throw a somewhat lurid light on the character and interests of the then Lord Stavordale, son and heir of the Earl of Ilchester.

George Selwyn was the chairman of a House of Commons committee appointed to handle a bill for the enclosure of Sedgmoor, in Somerset. It was being promoted by Lord Bolingbroke, who had property in the vicinity and was up to his eyes in gambling debts. The scheme was to enclose 18,000 acres of pastureland on Sedgmoor, involving some thirty-five parishes and hamlets.

All the usual arguments were advanced about the improvements which would result, reinforced by the accurate statement that in winter these marshy lands were, in any case, like an inland sea. What the Bill did not say was that Bolingbroke stood to gain a clear £30,000 by the enclosures. Stavordale, who was 'deeply engaged in the Bill' would profit by £2,000, which would be more than welcome, for, says Selwyn, 'He told me himself that his last trip to town had cost him £4,000'! He and Bolingbroke, compulsive gamblers like so many of their crowd, owed money everywhere. They were precluded from raising more money on mortgage on their entailed inheritances but could quickly raise new mortgages on land acquired by enclosures.

So Selwyn and his confederates did their best to push their bill through Parliament, well aware that that was their best chance of securing payment of the debts due to themselves. Charles Fox supported them, but unfortunately for them they met with formidable opposition, including that of the prime minister, Lord North. Moreover, the promoters of the Bill overreached themselves. They deceived even their own advocate, Selwyn, by sending him a copy of the Bill differing in twenty important details from that which had been circulated to the interested parties in Somerset. Getting wind of this discrepancy, twenty members of the committee diplomatically stayed away from the crucial meeting, and as a result the Bill was thrown out. All for the sake of 'a half-fed cow or hog, furnishing the means of adding intemperance to idleness', as a disgruntled protagonist of another Sedgmoor reclamation scheme put it bitterly, a few years later.

Whatever the indiscretions of Lord Stavordale in his wild youth, they did no permanent damage to the Ilchester estates, but obviously when, thirty-five years later, the Pitton and Farley estate came up for enclosure, the way through the legal maze obfuscating the passage of the necessary Act of Parliament was a familiar one. Although at that time the lessee of the estate, within the course of the century the earl became the sole owner of most of it. He was clearly a major beneficiary.

Let us look at the farmers. Thomas Davis's maxim that a farmer worth £200 a year or more would be better off and a farmer worth £40 a year or less would be worse off as a result of an enclosure is a fair guide. By that criterion and assuming that the scale of expenses relating to the enclosure is a fair estimate of the farmer's worth, only one Pitton farmer, Samuel Webb, appears as a definite beneficiary. He is valued at £215. Another of his family, Moses Webb (whether son, father, brother or other relation we do not know), occupied land worth £149. So the family can be considered well-to-do farmers.

Moses Webb lived in what is still known as Webb's Farm, in whose front yard an old smithy stood. He must have been a smith as well as a farmer, for the weathercock on Pitton church is attributed to him. Most of his land lay on the south side of White Way, on the road to Salisbury, though he was also allotted eleven acres of the former common land on Pitton Down. Samuel Webb's land consisted chiefly of a couple of large fields, 127 acres in extent, adjoining Piccadilly Clump.

Farming on almost the same scale were James and Thomas Maton, who lived in two of the farmsteads by Black Lane, destroyed by fire in the early 1860s. Between them they were valued at £220. Another member of the family, William Maton, had land worth £161. Most of the Maton lands lay on either side of Bottom Way, the new road constructed to give access to the enclosed fields and to provide a highway to Winterslow Hut (the Pheasant Inn).

Henry Cooke can be considered a substantial farmer, for his holding in Pitton was worth £191, including the lion's share, some seventy-seven acres, of the old Pitton Down. In addition he was allotted forty-one acres in Farley.

A considerable acreage was awarded to John Read's representatives. 'Read' is an old local surname, but nothing is known of John or why he should need representatives. Perhaps he had died recently. From the siting of much of his land it appears that Manor Farm was his residence, but he was also awarded the farthest section of old Pitton Down. He was worth £154.

Stephen Seaward had several blocks of land, worth in all £148. His was an enduring Pitton family, the last farming member of which, another Stephen Seaward, died within the author's lifetime. He was reputed to be the fifth general of Seawards to farm the same land, based on Bower's Farm.

Joseph Parsons, who probably lived in Cold Harbour Farm, should probably also be included, for although his land in Pitton was worth only about £19, he possessed several large fields in Farley.

Such were the Pitton farmers liable to profit from enclosure, and it may well be significant that several of them were awarded substantial sections of the old common downland. These were men who would most likely be approached by the Earl of Ilchester's representatives and their acceptance secured. The rest did not matter overmuch, even if they were inclined to protest.

We may take note of Edward Windsor, whose holding was worth £68, William Smart, £45, and James Parsons, £57 (though he had other land at Farley). By Thomas Davis's standards they would be neither better nor worse off.

And there were two other anomalous characters. One is the parson, who held glebe land worth £70. More of him later. He had the house and farmstead still known as Parsonage Farm. The other is John Jennings, who was an award of land worth £70 on old Pitton Down.

John Jennings was not a local man. His address is given as 'Evershot, Dorset', on the Earl of Ilchester's Melbury estate. And in the preamble to the Enclosure Act the two

commissioners for 'setting out, dividing, allotting and
inclosing the said Open and Common Arable Fields,
Common Downs, Common Pastures and other Common-
able Lands and otherwise carrying into execution the
several other purposes of this Act' are 'Richard Webb, of
the Close of the City of New Sarum, and John Jennings, of
Evershot in the County of Dorset, Gentlemen'. 'Each of
them shall be allowed the sum of three Pounds and three
Shillings for his Trouble and Expences for each day they
shall necessarily attend in the execution of this Act.' John
Jennings, who was evidently qualified legally, either took
his fees in land or helped himself to a little extra on the
side.

A moment of recapitulation. Our list of farmers who
could be expected either to benefit from the enclosures or
to be left with little to complain about totals twelve.
Twelve households which, allowing an average of four
persons per household, accounts for forty-eight souls.
According to the 1851 census, the number of households
then comprising the village was about a hundred, again
with an average of four persons per household. And we
have the testimony of the 1810 award that the
number of houses was then about a hundred too.

That leaves eighty-eight households, or between 300
and 350 persons, considered by the Enclosure Act to be of
little or no account. The manipulation of their familiar
fields and the upsetting of their centuries-old way of life
was effected without reference to them. Or rather, to the
legal mind they *were* consulted, for was not the copy of the
Act affixed to the church door, according to law?

To draw a clear line between independent peasants and
agricultural labourers at that date is impossible. No doubt
there were some who, occupying a tied cottage on a farm
or living, perhaps, in a squatter's hut, were entirely
dependent on wages. At the other end of the scale were
smallholders possessing a few acres of land which, with
their common rights, afforded them some sort of a living
but who were available for piecework on the bigger farms
at peak times, such as haymaking, harvest and hoeing. In
the 1851 census Elisha Whitlock (though whether the
same Elisha Whitlock mentioned earlier is impossible to

establish) proudly records himself as 'Farmer of 6 acres'. He is a survivor. There must have been many such in the Pitton of 1810.

As the law required, their interests were provided for in the Enclosure Act. A close inspection of the map accompanying the Act reveals three little rectangular plots of land, respectively consisting of 2.2, 2.16 and 2.6 acres, in the corner of the large enclosure on Pitton Down awarded to John Jennings. These were 'Poor Folks' allotments, provided to compensate them for the loss of their common rights.

They were at the far edge of the parish, and to reach them involved an uphill trudge of the best part of a mile. Though theoretically reasonable, the settlement must have been iniquitous by the peasants concerned. Perhaps, however, it did not involve much additional hardship, for they were used to walking considerable distances about their daily pursuits, commuting between those scattered strips in the open fields and retrieving their livestock from the common. Interestingly, when allotments were again made available under a new Allotment Act early in the present century, there were plenty of takers. These allotments, or garden plots, were situated about half a mile from the village, along Bottom Way, and were cultivated by village householders in the evenings. Bicycles were then in common use, however.

The allotments allocated by the 1810 Act did not last very long. The name 'Poor Folks' was remembered by villagers in the 1880s, but the enclosures themselves had long since disappeared. Perhaps they had had to be sold soon after 1810, to help pay the enclosure expenses.

6   Night Falls

Bewilderment and anxiety were probably the predominant reactions of Pitton and Farley villagers when news of the enclosure of their lands came through in that June of 1810. What will happen now? How will it affect me?

But haymaking was about to begin, and nothing could interfere with that. It was business with scythe, hay-rakes, wagons and two-grained prongs as usual. 1810 was a wet, cold year. Contemporary records state that, 'The hay crops were greatly deficient' and that, 'The price of hay rose in the following winter to £11 a load.' Haymaking dragged on till the corn harvest, and it was only in autumn, when the last loads of wheat and barley were safely in rick, that the new pattern of the countryside began to take shape. Men with rods and measuring-chains arrived and were soon busy marking out new field boundaries. Even then the impact of the changes was delayed, for there must have been plenty of work that autumn, planting the new quickset (hawthorn) hedges (many of which survive).

Let us look at the standard of living an agricultural labourer could expect at that time. Wages in Wiltshire were about 7 shillings a week, though in some parishes they were as low as 6 shillings. They were, however, subsidized out of the parish rates, a system which, initiated with the best intentions, produced tragic and terrible results.

We need to remember that this was a time of war. Following the French Revolution (in 1789) and the rise of Napoleon, Britain went to war with France in 1793. This happened at a period of bad weather which produced poor harvests. For instance, the summer of 1792 was '... remarkably cold and ungenial all over England. It was uniformly wet, windy, cold and dark, excepting one dry week in August, when the heat was so excessive as to cause many deaths, and at the commencement of September all thoughts of summer were annihilated by the severe frosts.' Subsequently, a commentator observes, 'The lamentable rains of 1793 and the several successive years caused every wheat sheaf to present a turf of verdant green vegetation, which one cannot recollect without sorrow or ever forget that famine in our land.'

Prices naturally rose, and indeed were to fluctuate wildly as long as hostilities lasted. In 1792 wheat fetched 43 shillings a quarter; in 1795 it was up to 75 shillings; down again to 51 shillings 1798 and soaring to 126 shillings in 1812 (the year Napoleon was in Moscow).

Alarmed by the developing situation, the magistrates of Berkshire met, in 1793, at the village of Speenhamland, near Newbury, to discuss what could be done. The logical conclusion, which they duly arrived at, was to link wages with the price of bread. They allowed themselves to be persuaded, however, that the system was unworkable. With prices jumping about like fleas, how could consistent levels be agreed and how could unwilling farmers be compelled to pay? They decided on a compromise. They agreed on a low basic wage applicable when a loaf cost a shilling. When the price of bread rose, payments were increased, but not through wages. Instead, they had to be supplemented out of the parish rates. This arrangement, known as the Speenhamland System, was soon adopted throughout most of the southern counties of England, with the most unfortunate consequences.

A foreseeable result was that the parish rate bill increased alarmingly. An example quoted by G.M. Trevelyan (*English Social History*) notes that Poor Law expenditure in Dorset increased by 214 per cent between 1792 and 1831. In 1813 the total bill in England for poor rates amounted to £7 million, whereas local taxation for all other purposes was only £1½ million. The reason for the examples given in Chapter 3 of the anxiety of parishes to get rid of any potential paupers is now evident!

Other consequences were even more deplorable. The system tended to drive a wedge between the larger farmers and landowners and the general village populace. How could it be otherwise? The farmers paid the lowest possible wages, knowing that the difference between that and a subsistence allowance would be made up from the rates. So the level of the rates was constantly rising, and the effect was that the smaller, peasant-type farmers were subsidizing their bigger neighbours.

A question that quickly arose was, 'What to do with the paupers?' To claim parish relief, a man had to report to the parish overseer, and the general ethos of the age was that he couldn't expect to be paid money for doing nothing. So how to employ him? In some instances, the overseer sent him around to the farms to work for what the farmers were prepared to pay him, and at the end of the week the overseer would make up the difference to the statutory minimum. Sometimes he went from house to house, working at each for a day and taking part of his wages in a meal. In one parish it is recorded that the overseer put up for auction all the paupers who assembled on Monday mornings. In others they (both men and women) were harnessed to the parish cart and required to haul loads of various commodities, such as farmyard manure, stones for road-mending and hurdles.

An even worse evil developed. It was naturally more economic for a farmer to employ a pauper than a regular worker on full pay. There was therefore a temptation for him to sack his full-time staff and get his work done by paupers. In consequence, when an agricultural worker became unemployed, he stood very little chance of ever getting another job.

An instance reported to the Poor Law Commissioners in 1834 illustrates the sequence of events that followed. It was of a hard-working, industrious man in Kent.

'He is married and had saved some money, to the amount of about £70, and had two cows; he had also a sow and ten pigs. He had got a cottage well furnished; he was a member of a benefit club, from which he received 8 shillings a week when he was ill. He was beginning to learn to read and write, and sent his children to the Sunday School. He had a legacy of about £46, but he got his other money together by saving from his fair wages as a waggoner ...' In short, he was a typical peasant who did quite well under the old system, before enclosure. But then he lost his job, through his employer's leaving the parish.

The consequence of this labouring man having been frugal and saved money and got the cows was that no-one would employ him, although his superior character as a workman was well known in the parish. He told me at the time:

' "Whilst I have these things I shall get no work. I must part with them all. I must be reduced to a state of beggary before anyone will employ me." '

The report concluded: 'He cannot get work in his own parish, and he will not be allowed to get any in other parishes. If he attempts to get work elsewhere he is told they do not want to fix him on the parish.' Naturally.

One other effect of the system is worth mentioning. The statutory maintenance was fixed for each man and wife, with an additional amount for each child. There was thus a bonus on having a large family, on the principle that meals prepared by an efficient housewife go farther with a large family than with just one or two. A man who was finding it hard to manage on his own dole thus had an incentive to get married – or, better still, to marry a woman who already had children. In consequence a huge increase in illegitimacy soon became apparent. As one witness before the same Poor Law Commissioners in the same year put it, 'The eighteen-penny children will eat up this parish in ten years more, unless some relief be afforded us.'

There were also ample opportunities for corruption. The overseers who administered the poor rates were local men, often farmers or tradesmen. What was easier than to arrange for friends to get all the best pauper labour or other advantages? Some estate-owners resorted to pulling down cottages as they became vacant, lest they be taken by tenants who might become chargeable to the rates.

The lengths to which some estate-owners were prepared to go to protect what they conceived to be their interests is illustrated by certain events in the decayed town of Ilchester (Somerset) at this time. An account of them is given in the Parliamentary Register for April 1819, when a member reported them in the form of a petition.

An election was impending, and Ilchester was one of those rotten boroughs which, with a population of less than a thousand, returned two members to Parliament. It was in effect, says the petition, 'the property of a particular family'. Apparently the proprietors were somewhat suspicious of the loyalty of some of their constituents and so decided to get rid of them by pulling down their houses. One hundred of them, housing 163 persons. Only eighteen or twenty of these unfortunates were paupers, 'the rest maintaining themselves by honest industry'. For a time they were housed in a 'sort of temporary poor-house'.

> Notice, however, was given, in consequence of prevailing political dissensions, that these unhappy families would be deprived even of that shelter. The parish resisted, and, an ejectment being brought, they were finally turned out. Thus 163 men, women and children from extreme infancy to extreme age, had been driven into the open streets in the most inclement season of the year. Some had screened themselves from the cold with straw and hurdles. Some had taken refuge in open stalls or in neighbouring fields; and a considerable number of old and young of both sexes, decrepit old people, with helpless infants and women in the last state of pregnancy, had been huddled together in the Town Hall, without distinction. The unroofing of houses has been heard of as an expedient of exclusion; but it remained for the agents of the proprietor of this borough to drive a man, his wife and five children from their dwelling by filling the upper floors with dung and filth, which oozed and dripped through the ceilings ...

The petition gained a lot of support but was finally rejected. Opponents agreed that it was a case of extreme cruelty, but it had broken no law. Where would it all end if a man could not take what steps he chose to safeguard his own property?

We return to our own parish of Pitton and Farley. How did they fare under the new order of things?

They had one advantage not shared by many parishes affected by Enclosure Acts. Although not situated deep in a forest, they were, in many respects, forest villages. Pitton can be regarded as the last village on the south-eastern rim of Salisbury Plain. Farley is a meadow village which probably started life as a forest clearing.

The forest in question was that of Clarendon, one of the great medieval forests of England. It was itself a division of the much more extensive primeval Forest of Penchet which once occupied much of the territory along the present Hampshire/Wiltshire border, from the New Forest almost to the Kennet valley. Its first documentary mention in history is for the year 1072, when King William the Conqueror called a council there. Evidently it was regarded as a royal forest, presumably subject to all the forest laws, at least from the time of the Conquest.

The meeting-place then was probably a kind of hunting-lodge, but in subsequent reigns it was enlarged and developed into a palace, covering some eighteen acres. Money was lavished upon it by a succession of monarchs. Artists and architects of international fame were employed to work there. In an age of strong castles, Clarendon Palace was almost entirely unfortified. It was a rural retreat to which kings came, primarily to enjoy the hunting, in times of peace. Henry VI was the last monarch to regard it as one of his principal residences. He spent the best part of a year there in 1453, during an interlude of insanity. The Wars of the Roses allowed it to fall into such a ruinous state that it was past repairing. When Queen Elizabeth I came to Clarendon, hunting, in 1574, a special new temporary building (something, one gathers, on the lines of a racecourse grandstand) had to be erected for her.

Excavations were undertaken on the site of Clarendon Palace in the 1930s with a view to matching the remains on the site, and particularly the ground plan, with the abundant documentary evidence. They were incomplete on the outbreak of war in 1939. When work began, the site, known as King Manor, was buried in a dense wood, and it has now relapsed into much the same condition.

A survey of Clarendon Forest made in 1273 shows the boundaries much the same as those of the present Clarendon Estate. Another in 1650 shows little change. Many of the place-names recorded in the two surveys are still in use. Villagers of Pitton, Farley and other adjacent villages still refer to Hunt's Copse, Fussell's Lodge, Ranger's Farm, Cock-road, Shreaves Wood, Carverel and so on. They can still point out the deer-leap, a deep ditch which, when surmounted by a strong, high fence, must have constituted a formidable barrier. 1273, incidentally, fell in the century which saw the building of Salisbury Cathedral, and much of the timber used in the fabric and scaffolding came from Clarendon Forest. In 1650 the forest consisted of twenty 'groves', each a mile in circumference.

Clarendon, being a royal estate, was regarded as extra-parochial. Salisbury Cathedral was considered to be its parish church. Old people living at the beginning of the present century used to maintain that Clarendon residents had the right to be baptized or married in the Cathedral. Pitton and Farley could not claim the same privileges, but the fact that Pitton, at any rate, was not mentioned in the Domesday Book is probably due to its being considered a royal forest village. The Domesday Book was primarily a survey of all the property in the realm for taxation purposes, and there was no point in the king, the recipient of the taxes, recording his own personal possessions.

A little later in the Middle Ages Pitton and Farley became associated in the records and administration with the larger village of Alderbury, on the edge of the forest a few miles to the south-west. The association is doubtless due to the presence in Alderbury of the Priory of Ivychurch, reputedly founded by King Stephen 'to provide religious facilities and instruction for the denizens of the Forest'. The community consisted of a prior and twelve monks, whose prime duty was to minister to the spiritual welfare of the king and court when they were in residence and to attend to the people of the forest villages at other times. This arrangement had repercussions to a quite late date. Although administratively Pitton and Farley were regarded as one parish, even the churchwardens' accounts and other local documents being compiled under the title 'The Parish of Pitton and Farley' at least from the seventeenth century onwards, yet until 1874 Pitton and Farley, as well as the hamlet of Whaddon, were ecclesiastically chapelries of Alderbury. Their vicar was the vicar of Alderbury, they themselves qualifying for only curates. An interesting sidelight on the story is that at the time of the Black Death (1348–9) the Prior of Ivychurch and all but one of the monks (or canons, as they are officially referred to) succumbed to the pestilence. The survivor, James de Groundewell, was duly appointed prior, when the epidemic was over.

Royal forests in the Middle Ages were notable employers of labour. Their staff ranged from wardens, verderers and foresters to minor officials bearing such titles as woodwards, agisters and regarders and, at the lower levels, any number of peasants who could be called upon to act as beaters and labourers. There is a suggestion that, although Pitton is generally supposed to have derived its name from a man named 'Putta', which means 'a hawk' and may have been his nickname, it could alternatively have been applied to the place where the royal hawks were kept. An arrow-head found near Bove Hedges in the present century was a barbed head of the type used for hunting and not a war arrow.

In the centuries when Clarendon Palace was flourishing, one of the most used routes to it was from Winchester (former capital of the kingdom) along the Winchester–Sarum Roman road to a point on the downs just north of Pitton. From there a track led along the crest of a hill direct to King Manor, the palace site. For many generations innumerable horsemen must have travelled this way. Men of the author's generation profess to have seen, or to have been told about, the apparitions second-hand, the ghosts of horsemen galloping along the crest on winter nights. Surely a significant example of inherited ghost memory?

The golden days ended when the palace fell into dereliction. The years came and went but brought no royal

visitors and the attendant lucrative programme of repairs.
No doubt many of the villagers found temporary
employment in building the elaborate grandstand for
Queen Elizabeth I on her hunting expedition, a building
reputedly constructed in a field of Queen Manor Farm,
Clarendon. Thereafter the estate changed hands frequen-
tly. King James I gave it to the Earl of Pembroke. After the
Restoration Charles II granted it to George Monk, Duke of
Albemarle, who parted with it briefly to Lord Chancellor
Hyde (who held it long enough to acquire the title Earl of
Clarendon) and then repurchased it. It went by bequest to
the Earl of Bath in 1688 and by purchase to the Bathurst
family in 1713, who retained it for over 200 years. To the
Bathursts therefore it belonged through the nineteenth
century.

When in 1650 the Forest of Clarendon was stated to
consist of twenty 'groves', each a mile in circumference, it
was a thoroughly tamed forest. There were fenced
enclosures, some to keep deer in and some to keep them
out, so that they should not damage trees. Trees were a
valuable crop, and so was the underwood which
flourished beneath the woodland canopy.

This is where the forest villagers had an important role
to play. They were the craftsmen who harvested the
underwood at regular intervals and used it for fashioning
a wide range of essential products. They were practising
an art which had been developed probably in neolithic
times and was certainly well known to the Anglo-Saxons.

Hazel, which grows well under a canopy of oaks, is
undoubtedly the most important underwood for commer-
cial exploitation. Much of its popularity is due to the ease
with which it can be split. A skilled craftsman can take a
slender hazel rod, five or six feet long and less than an
inch in diameter at its thickest end, and with a billhook
split it neatly from end to end. The split rod, very supple
and very durable, can then be used for weaving
hurdlework. Apart from the agricultural applications of
making hedges and pens for sheep and cattle, such
hurdlework was once used very extensively for wattle-
and-daub, the common material for the internal walls of
houses. Covered with limewash and then plastered, hazel

wattle will last for centuries and may still be found in old houses.

Underwood craftsmen harvesting hazel would cut each rod, with an oblique stroke, a few inches above ground level. From the stub thus formed, new shoots would be thrust up and be ready for harvesting after about eight years. Other woods which split easily and were therefore in good demand are ash, sweet chestnut and willow, though the intervals between harvests for ash and sweet chestnut is somewhat longer. But an inspection of ancient woodland will reveal that virtually every species of hardwood tree was formerly subjected to coppicing, after the manner of hazel. Elm, lime, oak, beech, maple and hornbeam were all induced to produce a regular crop of rods and brushwood. Ash was highly valued for the sides of ladders and for tool handles; chestnut for palings and hop-poles. Brushwood of all kinds was used for making wood faggots for fires. Interior fences in woods were often constructed to keep the deer out for the first two or three years after coppicing, to allow the new shoots which would produce the next crop to grow unmolested. An alternative method was to pollard a tree – that is, to cut off the main trunk at a height of about eight feet above ground, too high for a deer standing on its hind legs to reach.

Over the centuries a tradition had grown that the harvesting of underwood was the province of independent workers. The 'groves' were subdivided into plots of about an acre, each of which would, if the underwood had been properly managed, provide sufficient work for a skilled worker for one winter. In autumn therefore these professionals bargained with the estate-owner's agent over the price per section. On a well-run estate an owner might expect to gain a larger income per acre of underwood than from his arable land. Meantime the underwood craftsmen did quite well on the profit derived from selling their products.

This then was the salvation, after the passing of their Enclosure Act, of at least some of the peasants of such forest villages as Pitton and Farley. Each village contained an elite of skilled men proficient in underwood crafts, and men, moreover, who were known as reliable characters to

the estate-owner and his agent. Such villagers, having
spent the summer doing piecework on the village farms
(or sometimes venturing farther afield in gangs for such
specialized tasks as sheep-shearing), would have woodland work to provide them with an income throughout the
winter. They could survive the loss of their common
rights.

Several mud-walled thatched cottages which were
standing at the end of the century but are not marked on
the 1810 map are situated at the southern edge of the
parish, nearest the Clarendon Woods. They may well have
been built by a generation of dispossessed peasants who
wished to live as near as possible to what would now be
one of their main sources of income.

An analysis of the 1851 census, taken when things had
settled down after the upheaval, reveals ten householders
who gave their chief occupation as 'woodman' (though
one specifies 'hurdlemaker' and another claims to be only
a 'labourer in the woods'). Their dependants number
fifteen, giving a total of woodland workers and families as
twenty-five – not a large number. In contrast, the number
of those classified as 'agricultural workers' is 101, while
their dependants are 146 well over half the population.
The number of farmers in 1851 has declined to eight, one
of whom is Elisha Whitlock, with his little farm of six
acres. He describes himself as 'woodman and farmer'.

7 Goodbye to All That

The parish records of neighbouring Winterslow, which experienced no major enclosure, give an insight into some of the subsidiary occupations which helped peasant families to earn a living. An industry which flourished at Winterslow for much of the nineteenth century was that of '... picking sloes and selling them to the chemist at West Winterslow. The picking was done by families, great boughs being cut, and the children sitting all day and picking the berries off into buckets.' (Curious to know what sloes were used for commercially, the author has engaged in a little research. As far as he can discover, chemists used them in a very bitter purgative they made from aloes and also for adulterating port wine!)

The chemist (surely an unusual character to find in a nineteenth-century village?) also offered a market for the roots of the woodland plant valerian, apparently in demand in the preparation of a broth for invalids; it was also used in the preparation of poultices. Both valerian and sweet woodruff spread between the sheets in a linen drawer were said to keep the clothes sweet and fresh. Another poultice ingredient was the small downland snails, crushed between stones. Winterslow was also the centre of the truffle-hunters. In the mid-nineteenth century, at least twelve Winterslow families were engaged seasonally in finding the elusive subterranean fungi, and when dog-licensing was introduced they petitioned Parliament for exemption, on the grounds that their livelihood was threatened.

Hazel-nuts were considered a worthwhile crop, being of approximately the same value as wheat, for bread-making. Doubtless the nut harvest was of considerable importance in the peasant economy of Winterslow, and of Pitton and Farley in a good year, though these villages were not so blessed with woodland. One of the best accounts of the hazel-nut harvest is to be found in a splendid old book, *Anecdotes of Cranbourn Chase*, by William Chafin, published in 1818. Cranborne Chase is an ancient woodland region 'about fourteen miles in extent', on the borders of Dorset and Wiltshire.

> The Woods consist chiefly of hazel, which produce nuts in great profusion, to the relief and benefit of all the hamlets and villages for miles around it. It is their second harvest; for when all the corn hath been got in, and the leasing of the fields at an end, the inhabitants betake themselves to the woods; whole families from distant places flock to the Chase; bring their little cots, provisions, utensils, and every necessary for their comfort that they can provide themselves with, and make their abode there for whole weeks at a time if the weather will permit. Fuel they have at hand in great plenty; and after the fatigue of the day, they make large fires, which they sit around, eat their scanty meal, then slip from the green shells their day's gathering, talk over their success, crack their jokes as well as their nuts, and, clothed with innocence and simplicity, are much happier than most of the Princes of Europe, and may well join in the old song and say or sing, 'For who are so happy, so happy are we?' The neighbouring towns, particularly the seaports, are a sure and ready market for their wares, and the price is generally on a par with wheat ...

A typical condescending picture of life as lived by the 'lower classes' through the eyes of a cultured gentleman. In art it has its counterpart in the pastoral paintings of Morland and Stubbs. But in his next paragraph Chafin goes even better:

When the winter hath brought down all the nuts from the bushes and trees, some experienced persons still continue to get a store of the very best in a most cruel manner, by robbing the hoards of the industrious mice; and these nuts bear a better price than others, because the mice by natural instinct select the best, and no faulty one is ever found amongst them. Those are called Mouse-hole nuts, which are dug from the poor animals' store-houses; but it requires some sagacity and experience in the finding out the right holes in which the stores are kept; on this account the practice is now, I believe, nearly extinct; and I hope it is caused by the better feelings of the present race, and from their abhorrence of all kinds of robberies, even those of innocent mice; but I greatly fear it is not so.

As an example of inverted humanity, that would be hard to beat. The writer is overcome by compassion for the poor innocent mice but has no sympathy with the plight of his fellow men, driven by poverty to dig up the meagre stores of hazel-nuts accumulated by mice.

William Cobbett met some of these nutters at Heytesbury in 1826. They were unemployed weavers who had walked the twelve miles from Bradford-on-Avon for a share in the nut harvest. They were, says Cobbett, '... extremely ragged. I saved my supper, and I fasted instead of breakfasting. That was three shillings which I had saved, and I added five to them, with a resolution to save them afterwards, in order to give these chaps a breakfast for once in their lives. There were eight of them, six men and two boys; and I gave them two quartern loaves, two pounds of cheese and eight pints of strong beer. The fellows were very thankful, but the conduct of the landlord and landlady pleased me exceedingly.' Observing Cobbett's generosity, they decided to match it and so refused to charge him for his bed. Cobbett, delighted, comments, 'I must here observe, that I have pretty generally found a good deal of compassion for the poor people to prevail amongst publicans and their wives.'

Yet another wild crop considered worth harvesting was acorns. These were gathered from the ground beneath the oaks and used for feeding cottage pigs, though before the enclosures the pigs were no doubt turned loose to forage for themselves. The author remembers spending several afternoons in the early 1930s with two or three men shovelling up acorns under the oaks in certain fields on his father's farm. Although the acorns found their destination in the pig trough, he believes that the chief reason for the operation was to clear the meadows of acorns before the cows were allowed in to graze. Acorns in the ruminant stomach of a cow are likely to have disastrous consequences!

In neighbouring parishes, where oaks were even more plentiful, the acorn harvest was considered of major importance. From the edge of the New Forest the 1956 scrapbook of the Landford and Hamptworth Women's Institute quotes the log-book of Landford School for 1868: 'November 2nd. Am rejoiced to find that Acorning has ended for this Season and that nearly the whole of those absenting themselves on that account have returned to School this morning; having had a most bountiful harvest, such a one as the oldest inhabitants have no recollection.'

Then, of course, there were mushrooms and blackberries to be gathered in their proper seasons. To them, in our age of plenty, we might be tempted to add elderberries and crab apples, forgetting that in the early nineteenth century villagers at the lower end of the social scale would not have supplies of sugar for making jams and preserves.

Even if sugar had been affordable, there was a prejudice, in certain quarters, against using it. As late as the 1950s the author, taking tea with an old couple in a remote West Country village, declined sugar in his tea. 'Oh, be you a Wesleyan then?' asked the old man, referring to the Nonconformists who had refused sugar on the grounds that it was grown by slave labour in the West Indies, before the abolition of slavery in the British colonies in 1833. A not unworthy act of self-denial.

Modern books on diet extol the virtues of a range of wild vegetables and herbs, but most of these are used for flavouring and lack much food value. An exception is the stinging-nettle which, when the shoots are plucked in spring, can be made into a pleasant purée, a soup or even a drink or can serve as a second vegetable. The author, following the tradition of generations of village ancestors, still enjoys them as an alternative to spring greens. In the early years of the nineteenth century they were regarded more as a famine food. At the time of the Lancashire riots which culminated in the massacre of Peterloo (1819), when the cotton industry was in the doldrums, a writer commented of one of the cotton towns that, 'The wretches have stripped bare every bed of nettles within ten miles.' Taking a turnip from a farmer's field could be a matter for prosecution.

When food was scarce, there was no close season for anything edible. Compared to their experiences with humans from prehistoric times, birds today live in paradise. Gorging themselves at bird-tables throughout the winter, they might well reflect that they have 'never had it so good'. Even as late as the 1920s cottage housewives were well versed in the art of preparing common garden birds for table. The nursery rhyme's 'four and twenty blackbirds baked in a pie' was a common dish. Blackbirds and thrushes can also be '... roasted in a Dutch oven before the fire, being floured and basted with some hot lard or dripping; or a piece of fat bacon may be placed over them ... or they may be stewed like larks'. Sparrows may be prepared in the same way. So may starlings, but '... their heads must be cut off immediately after they are killed, or the flesh will have a bitter taste'. *The Wild Foods of Great Britain* by T. Cameron, published by Routledge in 1917 as a wartime effort. It is necessary to skin young rooks.

Even in the days before firearms became commonplace, men were adept at catching and killing all the birds they needed. They netted them, caught them in a variety of simple but ingenious traps, snared them with bird-lime, enticed them with decoys, killed them at their roosts, dispatched them with arrows or stones.

A story which had wide circulation in medieval England tells of the prowess of a longbowman who was asked to give a demonstration of his skill. His challengers were a party of noblemen out hawking. One had loosed a falcon which was about to swoop on a heron high overhead. With one arrow the archer brought down the heron and with the second, dispatched almost immediately, sent the falcon tumbling. One senses that the tale may be a little apocryphal, for even in the days of the dominance of the English longbow it seems doubtful whether an archer would dare to shoot a nobleman's hawk, but it does serve to illustrate the undoubted capacity of that fearsome weapon.

Nor was it the only one available. The author as a boy became quite proficient with a stone-flinger, then enjoying a vogue with village boys. It consisted simply of a supple stick from whose cleft a flat stone was propelled with a deft flick of the wrist. Considerable accuracy could be achieved. The device was an adaptation of the sling of classical times, and earlier generations, who handed down the expertise, were doubtless familiar with the passage in the Bible (Judges, Chapter 20) about the warriors of the tribe of Benjamin, among whom, 'There were seven hundred chosen men, lefthanded; every one could sling stones at an hair breadth, and not miss.'

As for netting, the lane in Pitton still known as Cock-road is supposed to have derived its name from being a site where medieval fowlers spread nets for woodcock. One is reminded of Papageno, the jolly bird-catcher in Mozart's *The Magic Flute*:

> I spread my nets and whistle clear
> And catch the birds as they come near,
> And from my cage they cannot stir,
> For I'm a jolly bird-catcher.

In the 1920s the author was shown by his father how to set horsehair nooses for skylarks and buntings on threshing rubbish, and how to construct brick traps for any small birds. Both brick traps and snares, and a combination of the two, were used for catching wheatears on the downs, in a season which began on 25 July. On the Isle of Portland, Dorset, much frequented by wheatears in the migration season, boys using these methods used to catch as many as 400 a day. They sold them for 3 pence a dozen, for the birds were regarded as delicacies. In downland Sussex it was the custom for poulterers to give a dinner at the end of the wheatear season to the shepherds on whom they relied for their supplies. No doubt Pitton shepherds had a ready market with the Salisbury poulterers.

Eggs were appreciated as much as birds. Lapwings' eggs were still regularly collected in the 1920s and were considered a delicacy and therefore saleable. Pigeons' eggs, however, were a poor man's dish; they were boiled for two minutes and eaten like hens' eggs. Even the eggs of small birds were taken. A nineteenth-century cook-book advises, 'It is easy to collect a sufficient number of fresh sparrows' eggs to make an omelette nearly as delicate in flavour as one made of the eggs of the starling.'

By the hungry years of the first half of the nineteenth century the hedgehogs which had been regarded as vermin in the previous century, their destruction earning a bonus from the parish churchwardens, had become a valued item of food for poor families. The gipsy technique of wrapping the hedgehog in a ball of clay and roasting it in the ashes of a wood fire seems to have been well known.

Rabbits were far less plentiful than they became later in the century. Though now wild, they were still in the aftermath of the centuries when they were farmed in warrens. Their real opportunity to overrun the countryside came from 1875 onwards, when the agricultural depression allowed great expanses of downland to fall derelict. In the early years, therefore, they did not feature largely in the cottagers' diet, and, indeed, on some estates they were reckoned as game.

Hares, of course, were protected game right through the century, killing them being subject to draconian penalties.

Any deer in the woods were fallow. In most of Wiltshire they were not numerous, though still to be found in some numbers in such wild regions as Cranborne Chase. Certainly there were insufficient in the woods around Pitton and Farley to attract either protection or poachers, though towards the end of the century they increased. Roe deer, once indigenous to Britain, became virtually extinct in the Middle Ages, and the present abundant population derives from reintroductions in the nineteenth century. They remained scarce, however, until recent years.

Badgers are edible. Those qualified to express an opinion

say that their smoked hams are very good. Throughout history, though, their numbers have been kept low by the demand for subjects for badger-baiting, and badger meat could seldom have been available in private homes. It was usually reserved for pub feasts.

Such were the foods of the wild countryside by which humble cottagers could at times eke out their meagre diet. Enclosures curtailed the supplies of some of them, at a time when they were all the more valuable as substitutes for the livestock that peasants could no longer keep on the commons. The type of livestock which now multiplied exceedingly, creating bitter friction, consisted of the creatures regarded as game.

These were primarily partridges, pheasants and hares, though corncrakes, snipe and, in some districts, rabbits were at times included. Until around the middle of the eighteenth century partridges were probably the most popular. The common practice of harvesting corn with sickles rather than scythes left the arable fields after harvest clothed in long stubble, providing good cover for the birds. Moreover the muzzle-loading guns then in use gave them an advantage. After each shot the sportsman had to go through the lengthy and tricky business of reloading, during which time the partridges flew far away, to the next field but one.

As weaponry improved, the toll grew heavier and partridges scarcer. The emphasis shifted to pheasants, which, however, were put up by dogs and shot like partridges, not driven as at present. The attractions of a fine country estate now began to include a pheasant shoot for guests. To ensure a worthwhile day's sport, large numbers of birds were reared under domestic hens and released, and a rapidly increasing force of gamekeepers was enrolled to rear and protect them.

One of the chief consequences of enclosures, therefore, was the intensification of the long poaching war in the countryside. The war itself was no new phenomenon. It had started even before William the Conqueror devised drastic new laws to protect his deer. Estate-owners taking steps to safeguard their pheasants felt they had the justification of long tradition.

The peasantry, on the other hand, argued that wild creatures were nobody's property. They were the legitimate prey of anyone competent enough to take them. And with enclosures their grievance was compounded, for they complained that, with the loss of their common land, they had also lost the right to capture and eat the wild creatures that lived on it. Poachers drew a firm distinction between poaching and ordinary theft. When magistrates examining a Norfolk poacher, Willim Gowing, in 1844, put it to him that a poacher would just as soon help himself to poultry or sheep, Gowing said firmly, 'Those are not poachers; a thief is not a poacher.'

Any rights or wrongs in the argument tended to be submerged by sheer necessity and opportunity. To a man who, with a family of young children, has been existing for a week on meagre rations of bread and cheese, together with any wild foods available from the list given above, the sight of fat pheasants scratching about unconcernedly at the woodland edge must have been indescribably tantalizing. When night fell, he would have one of those for the pot, if he could devise some plan for taking it without getting caught.

There is one other factor in the rural scene in the early years of the nineteenth century to be considered. It is an unprecedented population explosion.

When Queen Anne came to the throne in 1702 the population of England and Wales was around 5½ million. A century later it had increased to 9 million. Thereafter the rate of increase accelerated, and the biggest every recorded – from 12½ to 14½ million – occurred in the decade 1811 to 1821.

No one is quite sure about the causes of this increase. The historian Professor G.M. Trevelyan attributes it to improved medical service. When we reflect that such an exalted person as Queen Anne had seventeen children in the first nineteen years of her married life but that not one of them had survived at the time of her accession to the throne, we may concede that he was probably right. As mentioned in *The Lost Village*, village wives at the beginning of the present century would ask another woman not how many children she had *had* but how many she had *reared*. On the other hand, readers may feel that the immorality fostered by the Poor Law legislation of the early nineteenth century (described in Chapter 3) may have had something to do with it.

The effects in the countryside are not difficult to imagine. At a time when so many cottagers, dispossessed of their common rights, were having to rely more entirely on their wages as agricultural labourers, there were more of them every year to share out the available work. For the farmers it was a buyer's market. They could get as many hands as they needed for almost any wage. Every incentive existed to keep wages low and to subsidize them from the rates. As an American observer noted in 1830: 'The term pauper as used in England, and more particularly in agricultural districts, embraces that numerous class of society who depends for subsistence solely upon the labour of their lands.' A damning indictment. A farm labourer was of necessity a pauper.

The trend continued throughout much of the nineteenth century. The villages became overstocked with artisans and craftsmen as well as agricultural workers. As an instance, in 1841 the village of Bere Regis, in Dorset, had no fewer than eighteen cobblers in a population of just under 1,400. In the same year the village had four dressmakers, but by 1851 there were sixteen. How could they all have found work?

An alternative accepted reluctantly by many was to migrate to the growing industrial towns of the North and Midlands. What they found when they got there could not have been to their liking, but there was no going back. There must have been many exiled country folk who, like Wordsworth's 'Poor Susan', pined for her country cottage, 'The one only dwelling on earth that she loves'.

At this time the forecasts of Thomas Malthus were attracting a lot of anxious attention. As he saw it, a population inevitably outgrows its food supply unless or until it is checked by some catastrophe, such as famine, disease or war. In the first half of the nineteenth century his pessimistic warnings seemed to be inexorably working out; indeed, it was not until 1875 that they were nullified by intervention from an unforeseen quarter.

As Britain settled down – if such an expression can be used for those turbulent times – after the Napoleonic Wars, the prevailing opinion among the upper classes, including the more prosperous farmers, was that the countryside was grossly overpopulated. A relaxation in the severity with which poor travellers were treated is a symptom of this attitude. Instead of being whipped out of the parish, they were, in many instances (one of which is quoted in Chapter 3) helped on their way, provided they could satisfy the parish authorities that they were never likely to return and become chargeable to the rates. The pious hope was that they were on their way to the vast new industrial slums in the North, where no questions were asked and where they could expect no subsidies from the rates.

The situation also resulted in the formation of emigration committees, for which that old political firebrand William Cobbett reserved some of his most caustic comments. Riding down the valley of the Salisbury Avon in August 1826, he was outraged at finding, in the village of Milton, an emigration committee devising '... the means of getting rid, not of the idlers, not of the pensioners, not of the dead-weight, not of the parsons, not of the soldiers ... but of these working people, who are grudged even the miserable morsel that they get!' He adds that he fully expects that Parliament, next session, will be asked to '... pass a law to enable overseers and vestries and magistrates *to transport paupers beyond the seas*'. 'They are base enough for this or for anything,' he fulminated, 'but the whole system will go to the devil long before they get such an act passed.'

On his journey down the Avon valley Cobbett was sufficiently moved to engage in some detailed calculations of the economy of one of the parishes, Milton. The land in the parish produces annually, he estimates, about 3,000 quarters of wheat, 6,000 quarters of barley and the wool of 7,000 sheep, besides pigs and poultry. He then turns to the needs of an average family of agricultural labourers – 'a family of five persons; a man, wife and three children, one child big enough to work, one big enough to eat heartily, and one a baby'. Such a family, he asserts, would want

five pounds of bread, a pound of mutton, two pounds of
bacon and, on average, a gallon and a half of beer per day.
(He takes no account of green vegetables, which, he says,
'… human creatures, and especially labouring human
creatures, ought never to use as sustenance!'). He regards
the quantities he allows as by no means excessive: '… just
food and drink enough to keep people in working
condition'. The cost at prices then current would amount
to £62.6s.8d. per year. Yet at the agricultural wages then
prevalent (and he allows 9 shillings per week as against
the 7 shillings more usual in Wiltshire), the annual income
of the family would be only £23.8s. The lot of the
agricultural worker he therefore describes as 'skin, bone
and nakedness', and he reserves some of his choicest
adjectives – 'monstrous, barbarous, horrible' – for the
system.

Summing up, he points out that the farms of Milton
were producing enough food (on his allowance) for 2,510
persons, or 7,500 if they were to be fed at the same rate as
the half-starved labourers who produced it. There is no
reason to suppose that things were any different in our
own parish. The situation was aggravated by the fact that
the older labourers could remember better days.

For centuries the English peasant had been accustomed
to living pretty well. Daniel Defoe, writing in the reign of
Charles II, had remarked, 'English labouring people eat
and drink, especially the latter, three times as much in
value as any sort of foreigners of the same dimension in
the world.'

In Tudor times, when farm-workers ate at the farmer's
table, midday dinner consisted of 'not more than three
dishes well dressed', but supper, the main meal of the day
and served in mid-evening, was substantial. The
farm-hands expected a joint of meat at least twice a week,
on Thursdays and Saturdays. Sir Arthur Bryant, quoting
the budget of a Leicester woolcomber in 1795/6, says that,
although he had an income of only £47 a year including a
grant from the Poor Law guardians, he '… was able to buy
weekly ten pounds of butcher's meat, two pounds of
butter, three-and-a-half of cheese, and about nineteen
pints of milk, as well as potatoes, vegetables, tea, sugar

and beer. He was not even a particularly industrious man, for he was said to spend several days every month in the alehouse, lamenting the hardness of the times.'

But the next ten or fifteen years saw a rapid deterioration in the living standards of the poor. As already noted, the price of grain, and therefore of bread, more than trebled, whereas the level of wages shifted hardly at all. Moreover, in parishes affected by Enclosure Acts the number of persons now almost entirely dependent on wages dramatically increased. And although quite late in the century unmarried farm-workers quite often lived in at the farmhouse, sleeping in attic or hayloft and sharing the farmhouse meals, no such tradition helped the married cottager.

At the same time, England was enjoying a golden age, for such as were in a position to participate. The Age of Elegance. It is difficult to appreciate that Wordsworth, Constable, Jane Austen, Sheridan, Sir Walter Scott, Charles Lamb and Coleridge produced their masterpieces against the background of a wrecked Europe relapsed into barbarism and a grimy, industrial, urban England racked by the economic severities of war. However, a watchful Navy ensured that the physical realities of war stayed on the far side of the seas. Battles were exciting events to be read about in the newspapers, but hunt balls, summer picnics, race meetings, shooting parties and gossip about the neighbours and the royal family were the real pattern of the fabric of life.

Washington Irving, the American author, enjoying an English country-house Christmas in 1820, noted that the main dish was a boar's head, brought in on a silver dish, to the accompaniment of harp music. Additional dishes included sirloin of beef, roast turkey, gravy from fat sheep and a pheasant pie adorned with peacock feathers.

The cottagers, who had formerly been independent peasants before they lost their common rights, were aware of all this. Not only did their families provide the servants for the great house but they themselves were invited to visit their lord's mansion on special occasions, such as for performing mummers' plays or Morris dances. They were generously rewarded with 'brawn and beef and stout

home-brewed', but what they had seen did not help them
to be the more content with their lot as they trudged home
to their dilapidated hovels.

Sowing with Seed-Drill

8   A Countryside in Flames

Hard on the enclosures, a new factor arose to aggravate the situation. The products of the Industrial Revolution began to filter through to the countryside. One of their early manifestations was the threshing-machine.

The first English patent for this invention was obtained in 1788, and by the 1820s the machines were becoming quite common. In fact, by the decade 1820–30 Taskers, of Anna Valley, near Andover, were making them. They were understandably seen by independent farm workers as a deadly threat to their livelihood.

The erstwhile peasants, not permanently employed as carters, shepherds, dairymen or in some other capacity on the larger farms, managed to make a living of sorts in the summer months. They hired themselves to their more prosperous neighbours for contract hoeing, haymaking and harvesting. They formed itinerant gangs to undertake such specialized tasks as sheep-shearing. But in winter, apart from the woodmen, they had little to fall back on but threshing with flails.

All the barns in Pitton and Farley that survived into the present century (most were demolished in the 1950s) possessed threshing floors. These occupied the central section of the great barn, with tall wide doors on either side to permit wagons to be loaded or unloaded.

Wagon-loads of sheaves were brought in from the rick-yards, where the ricks made in harvest-time were being demolished, and the sheaves tossed on to the threshing-floor, where they were attacked by men with flails. The straw was forked out and loaded on a waiting wagon at the big door opposite. Other sheaves were piled at harvest-time in compartments on either side of the threshing-floor, from which they were tossed down for threshing as required, but none of the Pitton and Farley barns were large enough to take the harvest of an entire farm. The building of ricks was an essential alternative form of storage.

The flail is a deceptively simple implement. It consists of two short staves, properly made of apple-wood, though sometimes of hawthorn, fastened together by a hinge of eel-skin (which is practically indestructible). Grasping one of the staves, the thresher swung the other around his head and brought it down with a resounding crack on the sheaves spread out below, thus beating out the grain from the straw. A novice, of whom the author was one, would be sure to catch himself a crack or two on the back of the head until he got into the rhythm. It was hard, dusty work.

Stephen Duck, the Wiltshire farm-labourer who became Poet Laureate in the reign of George II and who once had earned his living as a thresher, describes, in what is probably his best poem, the attendant hardships.

> From the strong planks our crab-tree staves rebound,
> And echoing barns return the rattling sound.
>
> In briny streams our sweat descends apace,
> Drops from our locks, or trickles down our face.
> No intermission in our work we know;
> The noisy threshal must forever go.
> Their master absent, others safely play;
> The sleeping threshall does itself betray.
> Nor yet, the tedious labour to beguile,
> And make the passing minutes sweetly smile,
> Can we, like shepherds, tell a merry tale;
> The voice is lost, drowned by the louder flail.
>
> But we may think – Alas! what pleasing thing,
> Here to the mind can the dull fancy bring?

Our eye beholds no pleasing object here,
No chearful sound diverts our list'ning ear ...
... Tis all a gloomy, melancholy scene,
Fit only to provoke the Muse's spleen.

When sooty pease we thresh, you scarce can know
Our native colour as from work we go;
The sweat, the dust, the suffocating smoke,
Make us so much like Ethiopians look.
We scare our wives, when ev'ning brings us home,
And frighted infants think the Bugbear come.

Week after week, we this dull task pursue,
Unless when winnowing days produce a new:
A new indeed, but frequently a worse!
The threshal yields but to the master's curse.
He counts the bushels, counts how much a day;
Then swears we've idled half our time away ...

Poor threshers! Yet, uncongenial though threshing was, it *was* work. It offered a job when there was little else to be had. In the 1820s the village workers viewed with increasing consternation the replacement of the flail by the threshing-machine. No incentive now remained for a farmer to retain more than a basic staff throughout the winter. He could keep his carter, his shepherd and perhaps one or two other key workers and discharge the rest after harvest. The parish could keep them through the winter, and they would be available for re-engagement next spring.

For the dispossessed peasants, now relegated to the status of part-time farm-workers and seething with resentment and discontent, the introduction of threshing-machines was the last straw. In the autumn of 1830 they rose in revolt. The events of November of that year set the pattern for village life for the rest of the century – indeed, for the entire Victorian era and down to the threshold of our own times.

Little is made of the affair in most history books of the period, largely because the people most intimately concerned were not those who read or wrote history. Also because they failed. History is written by and for the victors.

A study of the newspapers of the time puts the events into their true perspective. For several weeks England was literally ablaze. Night after night ricks and barns erupted in flames, while well-to-do families shivered behind barred doors and mobs marched about, shouting revolutionary slogans and smashing machinery. Blood-chilling letters signed by a mysterious 'Captain Swing' were circulating everywhere in the countryside.

At least one mob was reputed to be marching under the tricolor flag, and the authorities were deadly afraid that the French Revolution, of some forty years earlier, was about to be repeated in England. Indeed, on 15 November 1830 Paris newspapers carried lurid stories under the headline 'Revolution in England'. On that same day the great Duke of Wellington, who in the weeks leading up to the troubles had been jeered in the streets of London, had had his house windows smashed on the very anniversary of the Battle of Waterloo and had been burned in effigy, resigned as prime minister. In sundry counties the Yeomanry, and in Hampshire the dragoons, were called out and were soon engaged in skirmishing.

The 'Swing' letters began to circulate in October, and the first case of incendiarism was reported at Canterbury on 28 October. On 9 November the matter was raised in Parliament by an MP who reported widespread unrest, an allegation which was answered by Sir Robert Peel with the assurance that it was all due to 'outside instigation'. By the middle of November the riots and fires had spread across Sussex and Hampshire, where blood-curdling threats were made against the Duke of Wellington, whose home was there.

On 26 November a battalion of soldiers was sent into action at Hythe, in Kent, and in Hampshire dragoons were called out at Winchester, Romsey and Fordingbridge. An armed band was threatening an attack on Newbury. By the end of the month the fires were burning and contingents were on the march throughout the whole of southern England as far west as Dorset and Somerset. In a battle at Tisbury, Wiltshire, a rioter was killed. By early

December the troubles had spread to Essex, East Anglia, the Midlands and the Cotswolds. A 'Swing' letter-writer was arrested in London. The prisons were rapidly filling with alleged revolutionaries, and everywhere new troops of yeomanry were being raised.

Beyond doubt, plans for the rising were hatched at the summer and autumn fairs. The greatest of these, Wilton (held on 12 September) and Weyhill (on 12 and 13 October – or at this time probably extending over several other days), were regularly attended by local people, notably farmers and shepherds, right to the end of the century. Other important Michaelmas fairs in the vicinity were Salisbury (22 October), Hindon (29th), Warminster (26th), Yarnbury Castle, Appleshaw and Andover. It was on the opening day of Andover Fair (19 November) when the town was packed with country folk, that violence first erupted in this area. Riots raged for three days, during which Tasker's Ironworks at Anna Valley, makers of the hated threshing-machines, were sacked and the machines smashed.

Occupying a place of honour in the author's home are three cups and saucers, from a tea-set his wife inherited from an ancestor. They bear a Chinese pattern, though in pink and other colours rather than the blue-and-white of typical willow-pattern, and informed opinion suggests that they were probably new in the 1820s. This fits in very well with the story that came with them, which is that they had been placed in a box and lowered into a well, 'to prevent them being smashed by the rioters'. Obviously a farmer's wife protecting a newly acquired treasure. The ancestor in question probably lived at Chilmark, on the other side of Salisbury, not far from Tisbury, where a pitched battle was fought.

The skirmishes in which the Pitton, Farley and Winterslow men were probably involved began on 23 November, when they tramped over to Winterbourne to join a crowd, armed with flails, clubs, forks and other crude weapons, marching down the Bourne Valley. Their first call was at Bishopdown Farm, where Farmer Colbourne had installed a threshing-machine. This they smashed, and they set fire to some ricks. The delay was unwise, for it gave time to the city authorities to organize some defence. In 1794, when fears of a French invasion or of an English rising similar to the French Revolution were at their height, the city had raised a troop of volunteer cavalrymen, seventy in number, including three officers. When the ragged army arrived at the outskirts of the city, they found that the news of their coming had preceded them. A contingent of as many of the yeomanry as could be summoned at short notice was lined up across the road by the Greencroft.

They were led by Mr Wyndham, a magistrate, who owned the Wyndham estate through which the rebels were now marching. For a few moments the two forces stood still, confronting each other. The magistrate proceeded to read the Riot Act, at the end of which he gave his opponents five minutes to disperse. When they did not, he gave the order to the yeomanry to charge. Some fighting ensued, but the labourers, in no sort of formation, retired to the high ground on their left, to a crest now occupied by Manor Road and Kelsey Hill.

There they fell to arguing. The bolder were for charging downhill and endeavouring to rout the yeomanry by weight of numbers, but the more cautious were by no means sure that they would win. Anyhow, their plan had been to present their demands to the magistrates of the city, and here was one of the magistrates, opposing them and clearly in no mood for negotiation. For the second time, a fatal decision was taken – to delay until after dark.

'The darkness will be ours,' they argued. 'We can wait for a few more hours.'

So, while some of the men stayed on the hill to watch the yeomanry, a lot of them dispersed eastwards to Milford, where they had a glorious field day, smashing machines, burning ricks and collecting guineas from frightened farmers. Others crept by detours down into the town and found their way to the numerous and familiar pubs.

After a time, the yeomanry retreated to the market-place, where they made ready to stand guard over the Guildhall all night. Scores of special constables were enrolled – citizens who were brave enough to venture out-of-doors. Towards the end of the afternoon armed bands were sent out to clear the main streets of the city, a mission reported to be accomplished by nightfall. They even ventured to empty some of the handier pubs.

What happened to the Pitton, Farley and Winterslow men is not clear. We do not know how many took part – probably only a minority. And not all joined the Bourne Valley mob. For Winterslow folk it was nearer to join with the rioters who were active at Broughton and Tytherley.

For any Pitton or Farley folk who were involved in the affray at Milford, a ready way of retreat offered through the Forest of Clarendon. But probably not all of them took it, for a large number of rioters assembled at Alderbury the next day, the 24th. Their ringleaders were captured when in conference in the Green Dragon. Fifty years later Pitton boys were told that some of their grandfathers went to live in Southampton for a time 'after the riots'.

The insurrection simmered on all through the winter. At Fordingbridge factories were burned down and a pitched battle was fought. At Christchurch the authorities unloaded cannon from a ship and made ready to use them against any attack. In the Blandford district 200 horsemen rode out to make the subsequent arrests, and the same number were needed to quell the riots around Marlborough. Farther afield several hundred special constables were enrolled at Dorchester, Wareham, Bath and other West Country towns, though at Horsham, in Sussex, only four men were found willing to serve, out of sixty asked for, owing either to fear of the consequences or to sympathy for the rebels.

By Christmas fires and scuffles were still occurring all over southern England, and the gaols from Norwich to Dorchester were crammed with prisoners; 270 were imprisoned in Winchester alone. But the trials were already beginning. An incendiary was condemned to death at Chelmsford as early as 13 December, the sentence being carried out at Christmas. The penalty for setting fire to a rick was death, as was an attempt to shoot at, stab or wound a person with intent to rob. For destroying a threshing-machine the penalty was transportation for seven years. Most of the death sentences in the aftermath of the riots were commuted to transportation, though six men were executed. Some 450 to 600 men were shipped off to penal colonies in Australia, the first convict ships sailing from Gosport on 2 February 1831.

The progress of the judges took place around the assizes of Hampshire, Wiltshire and Dorset. On Monday 20 December three learned judges, Mr Baron Vaughan, Mr Justice James Parke and Mr Justice Alderson, arrived in Winchester to open the proceedings for the Special Commission for Hampshire. They were accompanied by the Duke of Wellington, the Right Hon. William Sturges Bourne and Richard Pollen Esq. A Grand Jury of twenty-three was sworn in, ten of them baronets, three knights and the rest all entitled esquires and identifiable as local estate-owners.

To the Grand Jury Baron Vaughan addressed a lengthy homily, in which he admitted that, ' ...the low rate of wages to labourers in husbandry were a just and legitimate subject of complaint' but argued that, if the right to prohibit the use of threshing-machines were accepted, ' ... what reason could be assigned for denying the exercise of a similar right to those who are employed in the fabrication of cloth, cotton or any other article wrought in the various manufactures of the kingdom?' A foreshadowing of the arguments which would be used in anti-strike legislation later in the century.

At Salisbury on Christmas Day (no holiday for accusers or accused) Mr Justice Parke addressed a different but similarly constituted grand jury in similar terms, and on 10 January Mr Justice Alderson took up the refrain to yet another grand jury at Dorchester. To make the situation even clearer, Mr Justice Alderson ruled, 'We do not come here to enquire into grievances. We come here to decide law.'

Arraigned before this formidable muster of the forces of law and order was a rabble of prisoners who had only the vaguest idea of what it was all about. We have no statistics for Hampshire, Wiltshire and Dorset but a reporter covering the Berkshire Assize took the trouble to enquire how many of the defendants could write and read. Of 138 prisoners, only twenty-five could do so, though thirty-seven others could read a little. The ages of the prisoners ranged mostly from seventeen to thirty-five, with only eighteen of them over forty. It is safe to assume that the proportions would have been much the same in the other counties.

Many of them had been in cramped prisons for several weeks. They were brought into the dock in batches, having been denied access to counsel or to an attorney except in the presence of the gaoler. Not that a counsel would have been of any use to them, for in a trial of men accused of breaking machines or of demanding money, he would not have been allowed to address the court on their behalf.

It is interesting to read of the excuses they offered. Some seemed genuinely to believe that they had the sanction of magistrates or the government to smash machines. They had been told to. By whom? Here the evidence is confused, though evidently some farmers had encouraged the destruction, in the hope that it would help them to obtain a reduction in rents or tithes. Sir Robert Peel was undoubtedly right, too, in asserting that 'outside instigators' had been at work – witness the 'Swing' letters.

A common defence was that the man under investigation had been forced by a mob to go with them. For instance, William Cook of West Grimstead (about three miles from Pitton) would seem to us to have had a very reasonable defence. Together with Thomas Light, William Rogers, Henry Herrington, William Luffman and Thomas Gange junior, he was accused of breaking and destroying a threshing-machine belonging to Mr Timothy Rumbold of Manor Farm, West Grimstead. From the dock, William Luffman first addressed the court. He said,

> My lord, I was pressed into it. I was made to go, as I was returning home from a public-house with Herrington and Gange. There were thirty or forty men who stopped us and said, if we did not go with them they would beat out our brains. To avoid that, we joined them. I joined them, at all events, on my own part, without any intention of doing any harm. The beer was sent out, and I did not hear anyone ask for it. I am sure, my Lord, I had no intention of breaking any machine. I have a wife and seven small children, and I hope

your Lordship will be as favourable to me as you can. What was done, was done through ignorance.

When it was Cook's turn, Maria Rogers gave evidence for him. She said,

I live at West Grimstead, near to Cook, whom I have known for some time. I remember the night when the mob came to our village. I got up in consequence of the noise. The mob went to Cook's door, which was shut. They called, 'Cook', wanting the door to be opened, as they wanted some beer. He refused to do so, and they said, 'If so be they do not open it we will beat it down.' He kept a public-house. After a time the door was opened, and the mob went in. I was going as far as the door only at that moment, though afterwards I went in. The mob said, if he would not draw them some beer they would draw it themselves; but that if he would draw it, there would not be anything the matter. It was between two and three o'clock in the morning.

Mr Musgrave, who kept the village shop, and Mr Witcher of West Dean, for whom Cook had been working that day, both gave Cook an excellent character.

The jury found all the defendants guilty but recommended Light, Rogers and Cook for mercy. Mr Rumbold, the farmer, asked for the mercy to be extended to Luffman, who, he said, ' ... had always borne a good character and supported a wife and eight children by his industry'.

Next day they appeared before Mr Justice Alderson to be sentenced. The judge said that their cases had been accompanied by every species of aggravation. He said,

Your offence was committed when all honest people were in bed. At a late hour of the night persons were called up and the neighbourhood disturbed. You were not satisfied with destroying the machine but you compel the farmer and proprietor to give you straw, that you may burn it. You get drink and money and then impudently say you'll go to his house for bread and cheese. What punishment, under such circumstances, can be too severe? Some of you have wives and children, but you should have remembered those when you were about to commit the offence. They are pledges to the State for good behaviour. You have broken those pledges. The separation from your wives and children is a portion of your punishment. The sentence upon all of you is, to be transported for seven years.

The prisoners were then removed.

Though the sentences would seem to be excessive in every case, one would say that William Cook could consider himself particularly hard done by, for according to the evidence he was certainly acting under duress. It made no difference. The law regarded everyone associating with a riotous assembly as equally guilty. Incidentally all the surnames are of families still well known in Grimstead and the neighbouring villages until the Second World War.

Another local man deeply involved in the troubles was James Cooper, from East Grimstead. He evidently got himself accepted as leader of a contingent of disaffected labourers. He rode on a horse, called himself Captain Hunt and required his followers to take their caps off when speaking to him. He appears as the man in charge of disturbances not at Salisbury but twelve miles down the Avon Valley, at Fordingbridge, where a sacking factory, as well as many threshing-machines, was destroyed. The rioters then went to a local estate and demanded refreshments and money. When the latter was refused, they engaged in a pitched battle with the defenders. The Dragoons were called out, and next day Cooper was arrested at Damerham.

At his trial it was revealed that at the time of the riots he had been under considerable stress. Two months earlier his wife had robbed him of his money and had run off with a lover. Cooper, who had formerly had a good name as an agricultural worker at Grimstead and had served in the Army during the wars, had recklessly turned to drink and violence.

Of course, he stood no chance before the special commission. He was duly convicted and sentenced to death, as were many others, though the sentence was commuted to transportation for all but two of them. One was Cooper, the other an illiterate ploughboy aged nineteen, whose offence was that he had aimed a blow with a sledgehammer at the head of a local magistrate, knocking his hat off. No damage was done to the great man, but the offence was lethal.

In his initial charge to the grand jury at Winchester, Mr Baron Vaughan had emphasized that, dreadful though the offences of breaking machinery, burning property and demanding money were when perpetrated by agricultural labourers who thought they had a grievance, there was even less excuse for those who encouraged them, such as blacksmiths, artisans and the writers and distributors of the notorious 'Swing' circulars. These would be punished with exceptional severity.

An example was made of two brothers, named Mason, who were smallholders of the village of Bullington, in Hampshire. They bore excellent characters, were hard-working and had never been in any sort of trouble with the law. But they were intelligent men who took an interest in politics and subscribed to Cobbett's *Register*, which they regularly read in the evenings to twenty or thirty of their neighbours. Inspired by what they read, they had composed a petition to the King, pleading for reform of the existing system of wages and rates, and one of the brothers had walked over to Brighton, when the King was in residence, to deliver it. Naturally he was a marked man, and the judges had no hesitation in convicting him and his brother, on decidedly flimsy evidence, and condemning them to be 'cut off from all communion with society'; in other words, transportation for life.

The other category on which the special commission was particularly hard was, understandably, poachers. These were readily identified by the members of the jury, all landed gentry, and by the noble lords who sat with the judges, and they were doomed from the start. Towards the end of the assizes at Salisbury, when the judges were growing tired of sentencing defendants in batches, they let off one man convicted of destroying a threshing-machine with just three months in prison, but at the same time they gave another man, John Perry, a sentence of seven years' transportation for exactly the same offence – he had had seven or eight convictions for poaching. Twelve thousand miles away, on the other side of the world, was obviously the best place for an incorrigible poacher.

Predictably, Cobbett's turn came in due course. In July 1831 he was put on trial at the Guildhall, London, on charges of inciting the riots by publishing inflammatory material. Lord Tenterden, the chief justice of the realm, presided, and Lord Denman, the attorney-general, opened for the prosecution. What is more, the prime minister (Lord Grey), the lord chancellor and four other members of the Cabinet sat in the court, subpoenaed by Cobbett and waiting to be questioned by him.

It was Cobbett's greatest hour. Although the lord chief justice refused to allow him to put his questions to the assembled ministers, he had no difficulty in disposing of all the charges against him. Within minutes of getting on his feet, he had carried the war into the enemy's camp and proceeded to give them such an uncomfortable harangue as they had never before endured. The Guildhall was packed with his supporters – 'from every county in England', he maintained – and rapturous cheers punctuated his speech. The jury, though kept shut up all night, could not agree, so in the morning Cobbett left the court, free and triumphant. In the following year he was elected to Parliament.

The drama and the tragedy of the 1830 agricultural riots were staged against a background of profound unrest throughout England. The now huge and ever-growing manufacturing and mining towns of the Midlands and North were seething with grievances, one of the chief of which is that they governed by a Parliament in which they were not represented. Reform movements were flourishing. On 22 January 1831, when the commotion caused by the farm labourers' revolt and its aftermath was still bubbling, London papers carried an item from a Manchester reform group which pointed out that, while ' ... 102 boroughs returning 204 members to Parliament had a combined population of 186,370; Manchester with a population of 187,031 had no representation at all'.

Even such a hidebound government as that in office could not fail to agree with the logic of that argument. Sir

Robert Peel stated that he would not oppose a Reform Bill which enfranchized the big industrial towns, *provided* it was not extended to the rural constituencies. He would resolutely oppose anything as revolutionary as that. (The first Reform Bill was, in fact, passed in 1832.)

The attitude of the country landowners (and hence of the government) at that time is easy to recognize. *Apartheid* was not an invention of the twentieth-century South African government. It had existed in England for centuries and was causing explosions as far back as the time of John Ball, 500 years earlier. ('When Adam delved and Eve span, Who was then the gentleman?')

Apartheid was, to those in the top echelons, the natural order of things. It was not until towards the end of the century that the verse

> The rich man in his castle,
> The poor man at his gate;
> God made them high or lowly
> And ordered their estate,

was discreetly dropped from the children's hymn 'All things bright and beautiful'.

We return to the special commission of the turn of the year 1830/31 and to Baron Vaughan, Mr Justice Parke and Mr Justice Alderson assiduously convicting the batches of labourers crowded into the dock before them. Is it unfair to detect an element of sadism in the proceedings? Time and again a man is acquitted, taken back to the cells and convicted next day on an almost identical charge.

The judges did not hesitate to bend the rules. A small Hampshire farmer of good character was tried for organizing a petition to raise labourers' wages and, to the chagrin of the prosecution, acquitted. Thereupon the prosecutor wrote to the attorney-general, complaining about the acquittal and asking that the case be retried by another court. The request was granted; the farmer was tried and convicted. In a similar case, in which the jury were considered to be too sympathetic towards the men in the dock, a witness was found prepared to swear that he had heard certain jurors discussing the situation on the stage-coach bringing them to the assizes and alleged that they had said, ' … they would not convict in cases where the Labourers had been driven to Excess by Poverty and low Wages.' On this information the judge discharged the jury and empanelled another, hopefully more severe.

Said Mr Justice Alderson, addressing a batch of the accused after finding them guilty, 'You will leave the country; all of you. You will see your friends and relations no more. For though you will be transported for seven years only, it is not likely that at the expiration of that term you will find yourself in a situation to return. You will be in a distant land at the expiration of your sentence. The land which you have disgraced will see you no more. The friends with whom you are connected will be parted from you for ever in this world.'

Press reports emphasize the distress of the prisoners and their friends in court, especially the 227 who were condemned to death. 'Altogether, a more dreadful sight we have never witnessed,' writes one reporter, 'for it must be remembered that the prisoners tried during this Commission have not been persons usually met with at the Assizes – hardened thieves – but men who have been deluded into the commission of these outrages and who had before – most of them – been men of good character and respectable in their class of life.'

The tour of the three judges around the assizes of the southern counties was regarded by the inhabitants of both village and town in much the same light as was Judge Jeffreys' visitation by the people of Somerset, after the Battle of Sedgemoor. Shock and horror were the dominant sentiments – not at the riots but at the punishments which were being handed out. Nearly everybody knew personally at least one of the convicts, most of whom bore a good name in the villages which were their home. Even the dunce Henry Cook, who was hanged for knocking off the hat of Mr Bingham Baring JP, was buried with every respect. When his body was brought home to his parish, Micheldever, every inhabitant turned out to receive it with honour and to follow the coffin to the grave.

Petitions galore were launched and were quickly signed by almost the whole populace, including tradesmen, farmers, bankers, artisans – 'everyone except the Cathedral clergy', says *The Times* reporter, who further records that, 'The number of men who are to be torn from their homes and connexions is so great that there is scarcely a hamlet in the country into which anguish and tribulation have not entered. Wives, sisters, mothers, children, beset the gates daily, and the governor of the jail informs me that the scenes he is obliged to witness at the time of locking up the prison are truly heartbreaking.'

Perhaps in response to the widespread condemnation of the harsh sentences, the judges, having kept their victims on tenterhooks for as long as possible, commuted all but a few death sentences to transportation. They further added a strong recommendation that these prisoners be kept apart from the usual rag-tag-and-bobtail dispatched to the Antipodes in the convict hulks.

An open letter from Winchester, published in *The Salisbury and Winchester Journal* for 8 January, illuminates a new dimension to the situation. Having described the distress of wives and families the writer asks, 'The question then arises, What is to become of all these? Why, the only thing will be, that they must go and be supported by their parishes, the weight and burden of which will be very heavily felt. It is true that this separation is, perhaps, the most galling part of the sentence: but would it not be politic to let the wives and children accompany their husbands and fathers … It would be an act of mercy, and at the same time afford great relief to those upon whom the poor-rate falls very heavily.'

It didn't happen, of course. In due course, 457 convicts were dispatched in prison ships to New South Wales, and possibly more were sent at a later date. The greater number came from Wiltshire (151) and Hampshire (100). Many years later, in the 1930s, an elderly lady told the author that her grandfather remembered seeing the prisoners trudging down to one of the Hampshire ports, to embark. His father lifted the little lad to his shoulders so that he could see better, for a silent crowd lined the streets, four or five deep. There was no sound except the ringing of the men's heavy boots on the cobbles.

'Take off your hat, boy,' the father bade him. 'Some

gentlemen are passing by.'

By 1836 a new home secretary had given a free pardon to most of the convicts, extending it to all a year later. He did not, however, offer them a free passage home, and W.H. Hudson, enquiring about the matter at the end of the century, considered that no more than five or six of them ever came back.

A letter written by Colonel George Arthur, the governor, of Van Diemen's Land (Tasmania) throws a brief gleam of light on their arrival in Australia: 'I might instance the rioters who arrived by the *Eliza* several of whom died almost immediately from disease, induced apparently by despair. A great many of them sent about dejected and stupefied by care and grief, and their situation after assignment was not for a long time much less unhappy.'

There is, however, a brighter and more positive side to the story, which will emerge in a later chapter.

As with a violent thunderstorm, the insurrection produced what the countrymen would have called 'atterclaps'. Isolated incidents of rick-burning, machinery-smashing and plain robbery continued to occur. They seem to have died away, understandably, when the villagers had to get busy with the spring sowing.

No records exist of the struggles of wives and children bereft of their menfolk, though the story of the widowed Jane Whitlock, related in Chapter 12, must have echoed the trials of a previous generation. Life was now bleaker and more hopeless than ever. At the height of the troubles, concessions to the labourers' demands were granted wholesale. A report in a Salisbury paper dated 29 November stated, 'In most parts of the country it has been agreed to make a considerable rise in the labourers' wages. That this ought to have been done long ago, no-one can deny ... Wages should rise and fall with the price of bread or corn.'

No sooner had the unrest subsided, however, than reasons were found for reducing wages to their former level. In some parishes they were reduced still farther, from 7 shillings to 6 shillings a week. The attitude of the victorious squires may perhaps be epitomized by the action of a Wiltshire landowner who sent a servant to retrieve the ear of a rioter which he had slashed off. Later he had it mounted and displayed in his hall, with foxes' masks, otters' paws and other trophies. In Parliament Lord Melbourne proposed that the right of a landowner to set spring-guns and man-traps, repealed by an Act of 1826, should be restored, but the idea was quietly dropped.

The reaction of the alarmed authorities to the formation, a few years later, of a tiny embryo trade union at Tolpuddle is understandable only by reference to the events of 1830. Fearing that the troubles were about to start all over again, they stamped on it as on a tarantula. The remedy – transportation – was automatically repeated.

This time, however, it rebounded on them with a vengeance. The abuse of power was so flagrant that the incident provided a focal point for the young trades union movement and the agitation for parliamentary reform that was seething in all the big industrial centres. But it is ironic that the relatively minor episode of the Tolpuddle Martyrs should be so widely publicized and remembered while the major and far more formidable revolt of 1830 has been largely forgotten.

The role of the villagers of Pitton, Farley and Winterslow in this searing drama is difficult to establish. Geographically, the three villages were at the centre of events. James Cooper, a ringleader of the riots and one of the few who were hanged, was a man of East Grimstead, just a mile down the road from Farley. In the list of convicts the names Light, Cook, Rogers, Luffman, Herrington – all familiar surnames in the neighbouring villages – are prominent. Some of the major incidents occurred at Milford, Alderbury, West Grimstead and, on the other side of Winterslow, Broughton. Yet nowhere do we find mention of the familiar surnames of Pitton, Farley and Winterslow – White, Collins, Parsons, Whitlock, Judd, Pearce, Baugh and Horner (in mid-nineteenth-century censuses there are more than seventy Whitlocks in Pitton and an equal number of Judds in Winterslow). Were our villages really an island of peace during the storm?

There are conflicting clues. One is the reference, by old people late in the century, to a memory that, 'Some of our men went down to Southampton to live for a time after the riots.' It suggests that they had been involved and thought it wise to lose themselves in a big town where they could be anonymous until the storm had blown over.

Another, which points in a different direction, is the memory that, 'The first farmer in Pitton to have a threshing-machine was John Seaward, down at Bowers Farm, but that wasn't till some years after the riots.' Perhaps most of the farm labourers, not being directly affected, kept clear of trouble.

A third possibility is the influence of Methodism, Pitton and Winterslow having a strong chapel population. There is a tradition that the first Methodist preaching services at Pitton were held in the cottage of Jane Mills in the year 1801. The cottage, at the far end of Slateway, thatched and mud-walled, survived till about 1950. Jane and her husband, a mason or bricklayer, migrated to Pitton from Andover.

After her death there is a record that meetings were held in 'the schoolroom', though whether a Sunday School room or a secular building is unknown. However, when in 1836 a purpose-built chapel was opened, the village evidently had a flourishing Methodist society. 'The poor people of the village assisted by weekly subscriptions, and other friends came to our help. Thus encouraged, we proceeded in due time to erect a chapel on our own plan, eighteen feet by thirty. It was opened on September 30th, when a liberal collection was made. All the seats are let. The chapel is well attended. The debt will easily be borne.' (From a report written by James Ackermann, apparently a Pitton resident, and published in the Wesleyan Methodist Magazine for January 1836.)

Even earlier, a master boatbuilder of Lambeth, visiting relatives in Pitton, writes in a letter dated September 1827, 'We all went to chapel in the evening and heard a good sermon.' His hosts on that occasion were the Whitlocks, of New Manor Farm, Winterslow, who subsequently gave the plot of land on which the new chapel was built.

The inference is that a good relationship existed

between the farmers and labourers of Pitton and Winterslow. And the early Methodists had a reputation for being law-abiding folk. One cannot see them battering down the door of a public house and demanding free beer at two o'clock in the morning, as happened at West Grimstead.

On the other hand, a feature of the Methodist societies was the 'class', in which the members not only read the Bible and prayed but also learned to read and write. That was a notable step forward when, as we have seen, most working-class villagers were illiterate. It was not, however, regarded with approval by the ruling classes, who preferred to have to deal with an ignorant peasantry. It tended to produce intelligent and informed men like the Masons of Bullington, who read Cobbett's *Register* to their neighbours and were capable of composing petitions to the King. It produced articulate men too, such as George Loveless, the leader of the Tolpuddle Martyrs, who was a Methodist local preacher and was capable of writing, while in prison, the verses which became the marching song of the new trades union movement:

> God is our guide! From field, from wave,
> From plough, from anvil and from loom,
> We come, our country's rights to save,
> And speak a tyrant faction's doom;
> We raise the watchword Liberty;
> We will, we will, we will be free!

> God is our guide! No swords we draw.
> We kindle not war's battle fires:
> By reason, union, justice, law,
> We claim the birthright of our sires:
> We raise the watchword Liberty:
> We will, we will, we will be free!

Stirring stuff! Such a man was dangerous. Best to send him on a voyage of 12,000 miles, with the recommendation that, on arrival, he be set to work in a chain-gang, at road-making. (A recommendation ignored by a more compassionate governor, who assigned him to a job on a farm.)

If men of similar calibre from any of our three villages

had been involved in the riots, and caught, they would undoubtedly have shared the same fate. There is no record of any such happening. We must leave it at that.

Another factor, however, should not be ignored. As described in Chapter 13, Pitton and Farley, and especially Farley, were at that time better endowed with schools than most villages. The Methodists had no monopoly in education as happened in some parishes. The parish involvement is, in fact, surprisingly enlightened for that period. Did this work as a deterrent to the sort of excess that occurred at West Grimstead, Fordingbridge, Bishop-down and elsewhere?

9   Repercussions

The repercussions of the 1830 revolt reverberated down the remaining years of the nineteenth century, indeed throughout the whole of the Victorian era. In their effect on the everyday lives of our three villages they can be arranged into four main categories: the tithe system; poor relief and the workhouse; emigration; poaching.

The tithe system is marginal to our story. Its chief interest for us is probably the 1838 tithe award schedule and map, which offer an interesting record of changes between the enclosures of 1810 and that date.

One of the grievances which repeatedly surfaced in the turbulence of 1830 concerned the payment of tithes. Markets during and more especially in the aftermath of the Napoleonic Wars tended to be erratic, in spite of the Corn Laws which endeavoured to keep some sort of control over them. Harassed farmers, particularly at the lower levels, agitated for reductions in both rents and tithes, and, from the evidence given at the trials of 1830–31, it seems that some of them even incited the labourers to smash machines, hoping that the damage would prove useful in their demands to landlord and parson. Clearly tithes were highly unpopular and an embarrassment to rural clergy. The Act which became law in 1838 commuted the payment of tithes from a payment in kind to one in cash, creating a situation which, as it happened, caused a very similar agitation a hundred years later. But that is another story.

In the 1810 enclosure award for Pitton the official residence of the parson is Parsonage Farm, adjoining which he has fifty-six acres of land. He also has a barn and about 1½ acres of land at the far end of the Green, the barn being on the site of the present Glebe House. In his barns the parson stored the produce from his own land and also the tithes he collected from his neighbours.

Towards the end of the century an elderly man remembered: 'The tithe barn used to stand where Pitton School now is. At Farley it was the Black Barn, which is still standing by the lane to Farley Copse. At the time they were in use for tithes, farmers used to put ten sheaves in each hile. Every tenth hile belonged to the parson, who used to send his men to collect them. The sheaves he stored in his tithe barns, and he had to have them threshed at his own expense.'

He was, in fact, a farmer and employer of labour in his own right. The 1838 Act distanced him from his neighbours, and, in the case of Pitton and Farley, seems to have removed him, at times, from contact with them altogether.

(The situation is confused. Official histories, confirmed by directories and other publications, state categorically that until 1874 Pitton and Farley were chapelries of the parish of Alderbury. In 1861, for instance, they are so described in the post office directory, the vicar, the Revd Robert Hutchings, being resident at Alderbury. The Revd John Messenger, who resides at Farley, is described as curate, and Pitton has no resident vicar or curate. Yet at that time, and throughout the earlier part of the century and through the eighteenth century, official documents concerning parish affairs are without exception headed 'Parish of Pitton and Farley'.)

A close perusal of the award maps show that few houses seem to have been built or demolished between 1810 and 1838. Some of the farms have changed hands, however, several new names appearing. And as the 1838 map is more detailed and more meticulously prepared, it introduces a number of field names which otherwise would have been long forgotten, as they were not in current use at the end of the century.

Of much more immediate and dramatic impact on the lives of the majority of villagers was the introduction of the new Poor Law system, the focus of which was the workhouse.

Workhouses, or 'poor houses', had existed for centuries on a parish basis. Farley had a poorhouse in Penny's Lane. After the Reformation and the dissolution of the monasteries which had previously dispensed charity, they were the means by which parishes discharged their obligations to the poor, the sick, the aged, the handicapped and the other unfortunates unable to support themselves. The treatment the inmates received depended entirely on the attitude of the church vestries, which controlled the poorhouses. It tended to fluctuate erratically, according to the character of the persons in charge. Generally, however, public opinion supplied an ameliorating influence. The inmates were not anonymous paupers but individuals known to the rest of the village and doubtless related to some of them.

The Enclosure Acts, creating as they did a huge new class of paupers, imposed an intolerable strain on the ramshackle system. With agricultural labourers having their wages made up by charges on the rates, the greater part of the village population could be said to be on parish relief. Two years after the revolt of 1830 Lord Grey, the prime minister, set up a royal commission of inquiry into the situation. The result of its deliberations was the Poor Law Amendment Act of 1834, which established the union workhouse.

Poor relief was now to be administered on a national basis instead of being left to parish improvisation. The country was parcelled up into unions, each union comprising a group of villages. Pitton, Farley and Winterslow with about twenty other villages were allocated to Alderbury union. For each union a workhouse was built, though, for convenience, Alderbury's workhouse was in Salisbury. The workhouses ran to a pattern. They were great, red-brick, barrack-like buildings, very similar to prisons, and were promptly dubbed 'bastilles'. Their appearance was as repellent as conditions inside.

From the very beginning the new workhouse system was required to function in accordance with two conflicting theories which were, by their very nature, irreconcilable. One recognized that society had a duty to the unfortunates who were unable to support themselves through no fault of their own. The sick, the aged, the mentally or physically handicapped, the orphan: all had a legitimate claim to charity. The other grappled with the problem of enormous numbers of able-bodied persons, who, for a variety of reasons but largely as a direct result of legislation, claimed parish relief.

The latter was the principle foremost in the minds of the commission. The system of subsidizing wages out of the parish rates had, it was argued, encouraged labourers to regard parish relief as a right. As one commissioner put it, 'Industry fails, moral character is annihilated, and the poor man of twenty years ago who tried to earn his living and was thankful for it, is now converted into an insolent, discontented, surly, thoughtless pauper, who talks of "right" and "income" and who will fight for these supposed rights and income, unless some step be taken to arrest his progress to open violence.'

'Outdoor' relief was obviously flawed. The alternative was to offer 'indoor' relief. Those who, for any reason, could no longer support themselves, were to be invited to enter one of the new model workhouses, where they would be provided with accommodation, shelter from the elements and adequate rations in return for whatever work they were capable of.

The Poor Law Commission decreed: 'Where the pauper is the head of a family, and he declares he has no work, and proves satisfactorily that he can obtain none, either in his own or in any of the parishes within reasonable distance, he may be offered temporary relief within the workhouses until he can get some kind of work; relief, wholly or chiefly in kind, in the interval being given to the family, to prevent the necessity of immediately selling off their goods and breaking up the cottage establishment.'

The statement goes on to emphasize, however, that this is only a temporary expedient, postponing 'the application of the strict workhouse principle, which requires that all the members of a family claiming relief should enter the house and give up their goods and chattels of every description to the officers of the Union'.

And what to do with the paupers when, having taken the irrevocable step, they arrived at the workhouse?

Here there was indeed a conflict of opinions. Precedents were available. While rural parishes had been content with poorhouses before the 1834 Act, many parishes in the country towns had had some experience with workhouses. In some the paupers were employed at spinning, weaving, picking oakum, building or some other local trade. When a local industry was booming, it was even possible for a workhouse to make a profit for the parish for a time. The objection to that argument was that when an industry was prosperous enough to offer a reasonable living, no man would willingly take his family into a workhouse. His application for admittance was proof that he was totally unable to obtain work locally.

In order to avoid the union workhouse's being regarded as a soft option, the principle of the workhouse as a deterrent was enunciated: 'The Workhouse should be a place of hardship, of coarse fare, of degradation and humility; it should be administered with strictness – with severity; it should be as repulsive as is consistent with humanity.'

In general, these guidelines were effectively followed, though on paper the rules governing workhouses suggested model establishments.

1. To admit paupers into the workhouse and to cause them to be examined by the medical öfficer, and to cleanse, clothe and place them in the proper wards.
3. To read prayers to the paupers before breakfast and after supper every day, or cause them to be read, at which all the inmates must attend; but if any of the paupers profess religious principles indisposing them to unite in such service, they are to be permitted to sit apart and not to be compelled to join in the same.
4. To inspect and call over the names of all the paupers

immediately after morning prayers every day, and to see that each individual is clean and in a proper state.

5. To provide for and enforce the employment of the able-bodied adult paupers during the whole of the hours of labour; to train the youth in such employment as will best fit them for service; to keep the partially disabled paupers occupied to the extent of their ability; and to leave none who are capable of employment idle at any time.

7. To see that the meals of the paupers are properly dressed and served, and to superintend the distribution thereof.

10. To visit all the wards of the male paupers at nine o'clock every night and see that all the male paupers are in bed and that all fires and lights are extinguished.

A typical ration gave an adult male pauper, daily, nineteen ounces of bread, 3½ ounces of cheese and 1½ pints of gruel. Once a week he had eight ounces of meat and eight ounces of vegetables. On Sundays he had five ounces of bacon and eight ounces of vegetables. On meat days, however, his bread ration was cut by seven ounces and his cheese ration by two ounces. Women and children got proportionately less.

The master of the workhouse was expected to combine these precise instructions with the general principle of making the place as repulsive and degrading as possible. That the system quickly became identified with the second part of the briefing is made clear by the dread and horror with which village paupers regarded the workhouse for the next ninety years. Even as late as the 1920s the workhouse was a bogey with which harassed parents used to scare their children.

Soon after the passing of the 1834 Act England experienced an exceptionally hard winter. It started with a snowfall lying a foot deep on 29 October, followed by a blizzard on Christmas Day, said to be the worst for a hundred years. After two days from four to nine feet of snow had fallen, the wind piling up drifts twenty or thirty feet deep. The mails and all business were stopped for nearly a week. With no possibility of earning money by work, agricultural labourers applied by their hundreds for parish relief. But under the new Poor Law it was refused, unless they agreed to enter the appropriate workhouse.

From available figures, it appears that less than five per cent of them did so. How or if they survived is not recorded.

Apart from the trauma of having to dispose of their goods and chattels and vacate their home when they entered the workhouse, families fallen on evil times had to endure numerous other indignities. Though it may not have been general policy, in some instances old couples who had lived together for fifty years or more were parted, young children were parted from their parents, and there were even instances of babies being taken from their mothers, on the argument that having a baby to nurse would prevent a young woman from doing a full day's work. Such actions could be justified on the principle that life in the workhouse should be made as harsh and degrading as possible.

Illegitimate children were a special target. 'Base-born' was the epithet applied to them. Medical attention was denied to an unmarried mother in labour, except in dire emergency. Some Hampshire workhouses introduced a 'badge of shame', a yellow stripe which had to be worn across the workhouse-grey gown worn by all female inmates. The yellow Star of David, which Nazi Germany forced Jews to wear, was no real innovation. Pauper women could, however, escape the badge of ignominy by discharging themselves and their infants from the workhouse, and many of them did, preferring to take their chance in the world outside, which could hardly be less bearable.

Chronicles of the day are filled with examples of abuses of the workhouse system. Among the most notorious was that at Andover workhouse, about which books have been written. Inmates there were required to pound bones into powder for manure. Ian Anstruther, who has investigated the records in his book *The Scandal of the Andover Workhouse*, writes,

The smell alone was indescribable, making many of them very ill; fragments of bone flew in their faces, scarring numbers of them quite severely; and the plain effort of lifting the crusher for eight hours every day until they had pounded a hundredweight of bones, the usual quantity given by the Master, literally almost broke their backs. Even their children were forced to do it, little boys of nine or ten, who had to work together in pairs, holding a single crusher between them, climbing up on the edges of the box to obtain the necessary lift for the downward stroke. Their arms cracked, their hands bled; their sobs were choked by the terrible stench, their tears turned to mud by dust that clogged their bloodshot eyes.

One of the Poor Law commissioners, William Hawley, was delighted with the success of this enterprise. He reported with satisfaction, 'In one week after a Mill had been provided in the Andover Union, eight able-bodied paupers who with their families amounting to forty-three individuals had been a considerable time in the workhouse, left it on account of the undesirable nature of the employment.' Thus effecting a saving in the rates.

Worse was to follow. The starving inmates of Andover workhouse were reduced to eating the scraps of stinking meat clinging to the bones brought in for them to grind. The evidence of a pauper, Samuel Green, presented in a statement to the House of Commons, described what went on:

We looked out for the fresh bones; we used to tell the fresh bones by the look of them, and then we used to be like a parcel of dogs after them; some were not so particular about being fresh as others; I like the fresh bones ... the marrow was as good as the meat, it was all covered over by bone, and no filth could get at it. I don't know as I ever eat a bacon marrow bone until I came into the workhouse; I found out in the workhouse that bacon marrow bones were good; I have eat meat off some of the bones; I have picked a sheep's head, a mutton bone, a beef bone; that was when they were fresh and good; sometimes I have had one that was stale and stunk, and I eat it even then; I eat it when it was stale and stinking because I was hungered, I suppose ...

There is much more on the same lines, and the whole story was printed in *The Times*, creating a national furore. A select committee was appointed to look into the allegations and did so thoroughly. The Poor Law

Commission was abolished, the master of Andover
workhouse required to resign.

Harrowing stories innumerable, all well authenticated,
were brought to light in the evidence presented to the
select committee. Three children, under the age of six,
were fastened in some specially constructed stocks and,
though they were starving, were made to watch the other
inmates eating a meal they were not allowed to share;
their offence – bed-wetting. Another, aged only 3½, was
chased around the workhouse by the master and beaten
so severely that the cane broke on his back; he too had
soiled his bed. In another workhouse a married woman
was locked in a dark cell for twenty-four hours, without
food, water, coat or bedding, on one of the coldest nights
of the winter. She had offended the master by changing
the bandages on the chilblained feet of her child, aged 2½.
A mother whose 5-week-old child had died of bronchitis
was made to carry the little coffin for three-quarters of a
mile through the streets of the town and hand it to a
sexton to be buried in unconsecrated ground.

In the face of such abuses, which were widely known in
the villages, it is not to be wondered at that wild rumours
circulated. A Devon commissioner testified that there was
a general belief that workhouse bread was poisoned.
Paupers thought that, '... the only cause for giving it
instead of money was the facility it afforded of destroying
the paupers; that all children beyond three in a family
were to be killed; that all young children and women
under 18 were to be spared; that if they touched the bread
they would instantly fall down dead.' One woman,
obviously hungry, who was offered a loaf, put her hands
behind her back and shrank away, lest it should touch her.
She said she had heard of a man who had dropped down
dead on touching a loaf.

A Kent official said there was a story circulating in his
county, '... that the children in the workhouses were
killed to make pies with, while the old when dead were
employed to manure the guardians' fields, in order to save
the expense of coffins'.

After the appalling winter of 1838, *Blackwood's Magazine*
gave publicity to the same allegation. Tongue in cheek, it

suggested that, as the mortality rate and the cost of relief had been so high, expenses could be reduced by using the corpses of deceased workhouse inmates instead of burying them in coffins, which cost 8s.6d. Their bones could be carved into spoons and forks (amenities which workhouses lacked), their skins could be tanned for leather, and their flesh could be boiled down to make a nourishing soup!

Although the *Blackwood's* article was intended to be humorous, an anonymous pamphlet issued soon afterwards advocated even more drastic measures in deadly earnest. It proposed that the families of paupers should be limited to three children. Instead of strangling the surplus infants at birth, as happened with slaves, the writer suggested gassing them! A hundred years before Hitler! He visualized a kind of Garden of Remembrance, 'an infants' paradise', where people could walk and sit and enjoy the flowers.

These publications, like other attacks on the abuses of the Poor Law before and after, created storms of protests. Committees of inquiry were set up and duly reported. When the tumults died down, however, things went on much as before. Back at Andover workhouse the inmates now had to break flints instead of pounding bones. The chairman of the Andover board of guardians, the Revd Christopher Dodson, who bore much of the responsibility for the atrocities there, continued in office, unabashed and unrepentant, until his death in 1876. And the workhouses continued to flourish, if that word can be considered appropriate, for a further fifty years after that.

The story for the workhouses is entirely relevant to our theme. For the rest of the century they were the awful shadow looming in the background of everyday village life. The Salisbury workhouse was a very real menace to Ted Whitlock, the author's father, who is the chief character in the later chapters of this book. Only six months old when his father, a farm labourer, died, he was reared on parish relief and escaped life in the workhouse only through the fact that his mother had inherited, from a grandfather, the cottage in which she lived. So the system, by then moderated to that extent, allowed the family out-relief. But every minor domestic disaster brought the ever-present terror nearer.

'Oh dear! Now we shall have to go to the workhouse!', his mother would sob, on breaking a tea-cup.

Many a time the author has heard Ted recite the old jingle, chanted when the hand-cart which served as a bier bore a pauper's coffin to the grave:

> Rattle his bones
> Over the stones,
> He's only a pauper
> Who nobody owns.

Not surprisingly, the workhouse featured in the vernacular. A man with a face 'like a Workhus pudden jumped on' was the ultimate in ugliness.

Why did they do it, the authorities who devised and perpetuated the system?

A study of their attitude to criticisms, once the system was established, reveals a determination to resist any suggestion that it was in any way at fault. Facts were ignored, arguments refuted, erring subordinates supported. Authority is always unwilling to admit that it may have made a mistake.

To the poor, at the receiving end, the issues seemed plainer. They had no doubt that their masters were taking revenge for the fright given them by the machinery-smashing riots. Equally clearly, they saw the workhouse and everything associated with it as a part of a conspiracy to keep them in their proper place. They were the labouring classes, the lowest of the classes on which the edifice of society was built. They must be kept firmly in place, or the whole fabric might collapse.

As the century progressed, a kindlier and more benevolent attitude developed. The Victorian era is noted for the growth of philanthropy. The ladies of the country houses took pride and pleasure in dispensing charity to the deserving poor – expecting, of course, a proper appreciation in return.

> God bless the squire and his relations,
> And keep us in our proper stations.

Not all labouring class villagers subscribed to that point of view. Veiled or sometimes open warfare troubled the rural scene throughout the century. Its chief manifestation was poaching, as we shall see in a later chapter.

A curious fact emerges from a detailed study of the 1851 census for Pitton.

Out of a total population of 402, there are only five men and two women aged over seventy. And one of the men is classified as a visitor.

Of the men, one is a master bricklayer, John Mills, who would obviously not be a pauper. One is a woodman, and two are agricultural labourers, one of the latter being John Collins, now seventy-one and living alone. The women are Kitty Williams, aged seventy-two, living with her husband and an unmarried son aged thirty-seven, who is evidently helping to support his parents. The other is Ann Whitlock, classified as a pauper but escaping the workhouse because she is living with her son-in-law and his family.

Leaving out the visitor, only six septuagenarians out of 402 villagers. Why?

The census was taken right at the end of the 'hungry forties', when times were grim. It could well be that working-class villagers were worn out, by hard work and a poor diet, before they reached the age of seventy.

But a more sinister interpretation suggests itself. Had most of the old people been shipped off to the workhouse?

Mowing

10 Emigration

Riding down the Avon valley in August 1826, William Cobbett, consulting the *Population Returns*, learned that the twenty-nine parishes from Wootton Rivers to Salisbury were the homes of 9,116 persons, or 1,823 families. He had already worked out that to keep a family of five in good working condition on a diet of wheat bread, beer, bacon and mutton an annual income of £62.6s.8d. would be needed. What the Wiltshire agricultural labourers were then actually getting, on a weekly wage of 9 shillings, amounted to £23.8s a year, and from that they had to meet the expense of clothing, fuel and all other necessities as well as food. For families on parish relief income was even less – about 7s.6d. a week.

Getting busy with his mental arithmetic (how he could have used a pocket calculator!), Cobbett estimated that these 9,116 persons in the Avon Valley villages were producing enough food for 45,580 people, fed according to his ideal scale. But, according to the scale actually existing among the farm labourers, they were producing enough food to feed 139,740 souls.

At this his wrath boiled over. 'And yet,' he exploded, 'there is an Emigration Committee sitting to devise means of getting rid, not of the idlers, not of the pensioners, not of the dead-weight, not of the soldiers – but to devise of getting rid of *these working people*, who are grudged even the miserable morsel they get ...' And after long paragraphs of fulminations against the 'country gentry', whom he blamed for this state of affairs, he notes that, 'They will, next session, urge the Parliament to pass a law to enable overseers and vestries and magistrates *to transport paupers beyond the seas*! They are base enough for this, or for anything; but the whole system will go to the devil long before they will get such an act passed ...'

In fact, such an Act of Parliament was not necessary. The statute book catalogued a sufficient number of minor crimes, such as stealing goods above the value of one shilling, setting fire to underwood, stealing roots or plants, and getting married clandestinely, punishable by transportation to depopulate the countryside if magistrates were so minded. And from 1786 onwards, when Botany Bay was established as a penal settlement, magistrates were increasingly so minded. The emigration committees Cobbett so vigorously castigated had their eyes on Canada, but by the 1830s Australia was providing an attractive alternative, not least of its attractions being the fact that it was even farther away from the shores of Britain.

Little is known of the ultimate fate of the convicts dispatched to Australia as a result of the 1830 riots. Nor are the subsequent adventures of the Tolpuddle Martyrs a valid guide to the general sequence of events, for an unprecedented campaign back in Britain demanded their release and pardon.

However, there does survive a letter written on 15 June 1835 by a convict, Thomas Tingley, to his father and mother who were still living in his birthplace, the village of Newick, in Sussex. For what offence he was transported we do not know, but he seems to have been quite a decent sort of chap, and his letter throws a much more favourable light on conditions in Australia than we might otherwise have suspected.

Dear Mother and Father,
This comes with my kind love to you, hoping to find you in good health as, thank God, it leaves me at present very

comfortable indeed. I have a place at a farmhouse, and I have got a good master, which I am a great deal more comfortable than I expected. I works the same as I were at home; I have plenty to eat and drink, thank God for it. I am allowed two ounces of tea, one pound of sugar, 12 pounds of meat, 10 pounds and a half of flour, two ounces of tobacco, the week; three pairs of shoes, two suits of clothes, four shirts, a year; that is the allowance from the Government. But we have as much to eat as we like, as some masters are a great deal better than others. All a man has got to mind is to keep a still tongue in his head and do his master's duty, and then he is looked upon as if he were at home ...

This country is far before England in everything, both for work and money. Of a night, after I have done my work, I have a chance to make a few shillings; I can go out hunting or shooting of kangaroo, that is about the size of a sheep, or ducks, or swans, tigers, tiger-cats or native cats; there is nothing that will hurt a man but a snake; they are about five or six feet long, but they will get away if they can. I have dogs and a gun of my own ...

Dear mother and father I have eight years to serve with my master, and then I shall have a ticket of relief, that is to work for myself, and then to keep that for four years if no trouble and to have my emancipation, that is to be a free man in this country. I am now a prisoner then in this place, and then after that I shall have my free pardon to come to England once more. But I should be a deal more comfortable if you could get the parish to send you out, as it would be the making of you if they would pay your passage over, and give you about £60 to land with, you would do well. A farming man gets five shillings a day at day-work; if you was to come you could take me off Government for £1 for eight years to work for you, and then we should be more comfortable than ever we have been, as I am a prisoner; so I hope you will do your best endeavour to come to this country, as it is far before England ...

Please to send me word how to farm hops from the beginning to the ending ...

So no more for the present from your loving, though unfortunate,

Henry Tingley.

Another convict, William Stanbury, a Devonshire man, was transported for theft (he stole a horse) in 1828. He served out his sentence until 1844, when he was granted a free pardon. He was not, however, permitted to return to Britain, as he wished, and so went to South Australia, a new colony of free settlers, without convicts. There he bought eighty-three acres of land at £1 an acre and by 1853 was prosperous enough to build a stone house on it. In that year he was joined by his daughter and her husband, free emigrants from Britain, who started their own farm. When he died in 1858, he left an estate worth £300.

Stories such as these, filtering back home to Britain, opened new horizons for the harassed peasantry.

The insularity of village life in the first half of the nineteenth century is difficult for us to imagine. While drovers trod the old green ways of England, driving flocks and herds on foot to distant markets, and while soldiers, voluntarily or conscripted, departed to fight battles in alien lands, most villagers lived out their lives within their parish boundaries.

It was in 1826 that Cobbett, lost in the lanes along the Wiltshire/Hampshire border north of Andover, encountered a woman in a cottage garden near Tangley. She was, he judged, aged about thirty and had two children with her. He asked her the way to Ludgershall, which was not more than four miles away, and she didn't know. She had never been there, nor to Andover (six miles away), nor to Marlborough (nine miles away). The limits of her travels, from the cottage in which she was born, had been 'up in the parish and over to Chute'. About 2½ miles.

Cobbett was most impressed and rounded off his account of the episode with a few further examples from his experience. The author cannot resist adding one of his own. Visiting the Isle of Man in the early 1950s, he met a lady whose mother had lived all her life on the island without ever once seeing the sea! There is only one parish in the Isle of Man that lacks a section of sea coast, and that is where she spent her life. She never even went down to the town of Douglas.

It will be noted that these two anecdotes concern women. Men were more likely to be called upon to make a journey or two, in the course of work or business, at some time during their lives. A woman's place was in the home. There was no reason for her to step far outside it. Even in the more enlightened days towards the end of the century, village housewives in Pitton and Farley customarily visited Salisbury, their market town, only twice a year. Once at Easter, to renew their wardrobe, and in autumn, for Salisbury Fair, held about 18 October. Even so, pious mothers tended to forgo the pleasures of the fair, as an example to their growing daughters, whom they tried to shelter from the temptations of the wicked city! And as for clothes, the village carrier was used to taking notes to the city drapers and bringing home, on sale or return, parcels of even the most intimate feminine garments. So there was really no need for a conscientious housewife to go to town at all.

In the earlier years of the century the trauma of losing a man by transportation to a foreign country must have been shattering, even apart from the immediate anxieties of trying to keep the home together and feeding the children. It was the equivalent of a death sentence.

The transportations which were the aftermath of the 1830 rising, however, achieved for the blinkered authorities who managed rural affairs more than all their emigration committees had been able to do. For the committees, emigration meant crossing the Atlantic, for which there had been numerous precedents over the past two centuries. As a matter of fact, two Salisbury families with close connections with Pitton and Farley, the Webbs and the Whitlocks, were among the earliest settlers of Massachusetts. As early as 1629 Francis Webb, whose grandfather had been mayor of Salisbury in 1560, had been granted permission to set up a sawmill at Salem. The earliest land records of Salem show the Webbs, Whitlocks and Cromwells owning adjacent plots of land. The families intermarried and their descendants founded the shipbuilding industry of Massachusetts.

By the first decades of the nineteenth century, however, interest in emigration to America had declined, largely because a now independent America was for a short time in 1812 at war with Britain. Now the opening of Australia and Canada offered attractive alternatives as new homelands.

In spite of the great voyages of exploration in the seventeenth and eighteenth centuries, knowledge of our planet was still somewhat rudimentary. Among my possessions is an *Arrowsmith's Atlas,* published in 1842, from which my father and probably my grandfather were introduced to geography at school. It has been badly defaced by generations of children with coloured chalks and pencils and a penchant for comic portraiture but, for all that, is full of interest.

Germany and Italy are a mosaic of colour, indicating their division into dozens of independent principalities, the unifying work of Bismarck and Garibaldi respectively still incubated in the future. In England towns such as Old Sarum are in large block capitals, whereas Bournemouth is in the smallest possible type and written thus: 'BourneMth'. The coastlines of parts of New Zealand and New Guinea are composed of disconnected lines, signifying that these regions had not yet been properly mapped, and the only town in Australia is Sydney. The interior of Africa is blank, save for a few names in capital letters, such as 'EQUATOR' and 'MOUNTAINS OF THE MOON' – which last might have been anywhere within a radius of a thousand miles. There is also a vague name 'Great Marsh', and another, 'Negroes', and a dotted line called 'Park's Theory' (presumably referring to the explorer Mungo Park), showing how the Congo was supposed to link up with the Niger and the Nile somewhere in the interior of Africa. The United States of America do not extend beyond of the Mississippi, and cities such as Chicago, St Louis and Los Angeles have yet to be born. The name 'Snake Indians' in the Far West is 300 miles long.

But as the century advanced, places which were just names on a map began to assume a relevant reality. Distant Australia in particular became recognized as a place to which people might go – and, what is more, come back if they wanted to. Moreover it was, by accounts now filtering through, a pleasant enough land, where a man might do better than in England.

By the middle of the century emigration to Australia from Wiltshire villages was becoming commonplace. One name of which we have a record is Levi Collins, who was still alive, aged seventy-eight, in South Australia in 1896. He is known to have emigrated from Pitton at the age of thirty-three in 1851. The facts about him are known because in his old age he was involved in a legal matter concerning the tenancy of cottages in Pitton.

A migration which probably made a deeper impact on life in Pitton was that of the Matons, in the 1860s. In the village surveys of 1810 and 1838 the Matons are prominent farmers. There are three of them, William, Thomas and James, occupying some of the best land in the parish. But in the 1851 census only one Maton appears. He is Henry Maton, aged nineteen, living with his 23-year-old sister, Thirzah, on the family farm. Presumably his father and uncles or whoever they were had died, leaving him to carry on. He is recorded as having 320 acres and employing twelve labourers.

As already briefly mentioned, in 1863 or 1864 a fire destroyed much of the centre of Pitton. It is said to have been started one dinner-hour by some boys playing in a barn and soon took hold, fanned by a strong east wind. It was remembered, seventy years later, that sparks and 'flonkers' from the fire fell in Salisbury market-place. Two farmsteads, with a complex of buildings, barns and a number of cottages, were entirely destroyed. Neither was ever rebuilt. One of them was the home of a widow lady, Mrs Ainsworth, whose subsequent history is unknown. The other was the Maton farm, and it is remembered that Henry and his sister emigrated to Australia. An associated memory is that he took several of his farm workers with him.

Some of them may have been the Comptons. Compton is an old Pitton name, which occurs several times in the 1851 census. But at the end of the century only one individual was left. He was a little, black-bearded runt of a man, living alone in a tiny cottage and the frequent butt of jokes by unfeeling boys, for he was afflicted by a prodigious stammer. Sometimes, when he was tormented beyond endurance, he would retort, 'I've b-b-b-b-b-bluddy well had 'nuff. I b-b-b-b-be gwaine to Tasmannia!' Tasmania was presumably where the rest of the family had gone.

After the middle of the century a new migration of nations, from the rest of Europe as well as Britain, poured into America and trekked westwards. Canada took its share of this tidal wave of people, and the great impetus for the settlement of western Canada was provided by the construction of the Canadian Pacific Railway in the 1870s. To that epoch belongs the last chapter of this book.

Ploughing

11   The Poachers

The author's father, reminiscing, once told him of an evening when, standing on the brow of the escarpment on the southern edge of the Pitton valley, he heard the explosive call of a cock pheasant flying up into a tree to roost on the other side of the valley. Within minutes he saw no fewer than five figures approaching the tree, an isolated spruce, by creeping cautiously and surreptitiously along hedges from five directions. Presently he heard a single shot, but every figure had disappeared. He saw no one retrieve the bird, though doubtless someone did.

This must have been in the last decade of the nineteenth century or the first of the twentieth. Poaching was by then no longer an offence of the utmost magnitude, inviting draconian penalties if detected, as it had been for most of the nineteenth century. It was still widely practised, having been an obsession with generations of villagers, but Ted Whitlock referred to the episode light-heartedly, as though it were a bit of a joke. His grandfather would not have done so.

The poaching of deer had flourished from time immemorial and was still practised wherever deer were sufficiently plentiful. As late as 1816 the last of a long series of deer-poaching affrays, in which both sides carried firearms, occurred in Cranborne Chase, not thirty miles from our villages. Wounds were inflicted, and the two poachers caught were transported for seven years. In the woods around Pitton, Farley and Winterslow, however, deer were at this time too scarce to be of much interest. In Victorian times their place in the rural economy had been taken by pheasants.

So pheasants multiplied. Their eggs were hatched in large numbers under broody hens, and the cosseted chicks tempted with chopped boiled eggs mixed with breadcrumbs, with ant eggs, maggots and any other delicacies which the keepers who had charge of them could devise. As they gained their feathers, they were trained to come flocking for a feed of the best grain at the summons of a keeper's whistle. But they still retained some of their wildness. As they attained their full plumage, they were afflicted by wanderlust, and their wanderings took no account of man-made boundaries. Indeed, they obeyed the well-established law that 'Nature abhors a vacuum.' An efficient estate-owner who stocked his fields and woods to capacity could do little to prevent his expensive birds from straying to the property of a feckless neighbour. Nor into the gardens and paddocks of cottagers. And once off the home estate, who could testify to the ownership of any particular bird?

So, as has been made clear in previous chapters, the need was there: the greater part of the population of the countryside went hungry much of the time. The temptation was there. And the erstwhile peasantry considered that the moral justification was there, for had not encroaching landlords robbed them, by enclosing common land, of their natural heritage? No wonder that poaching remained, for the entire century, a major source of friction between country gentry and the general village populace.

However, the clandestine war went far beyond the simple taking of an occasional pheasant or hare for the pot. From quite early in the century it assumed the status of a major rural industry, operating according to the law of supply and demand. The market consisted of hotels, colleges, clubs and other establishments at which game-preserving gentry when in town expected to dine as well as at home, if not better. The Duke of Wellington, an advocate for the retention of the man-trap and spring-gun against poachers, recognized the ambiguity of the attitude of his fellow landowners when he wrote: 'The poulterers of London refuse to buy pheasants killed by the gun. They must have been snared in order to suit their customers! Very soon they will require that they should all be hen pheasants!'

And at the pinnacle was the Lord Mayor of London's banquet at the Mansion House, which required that the birds served should contain no shot. In other words, they were poached! An expression was soon coined and achieved wide currency: such pheasants were 'bagged with a silver gun'.

Most country inns on stage-coach routes did service as collecting-centres for game. It has been said that stage-coaches arriving in London carried far more dead passengers than live ones, the carcases being usually concealed under piles of luggage. Pheasants, partridges, hares and eggs poured into stage-coach inns from the surrounding farms and villages. Poachers made a far better living than farm-workers confining themselves to legitimate activities.

Writing in *The Autobiography of a Working Man* in 1862, the Hon. Eleanor Eden relates the true story of a young man who began his married life in the depths of poverty: 'He had got nothing in the house after he had paid the parson – no knives, no forks and never a table – no chairs but only one stool – and they had to lie in the straw. All he had was a pocket-knife and fourpence halfpenny. He asked his wife what he had better do – buy a loaf of bread or fourpennorth of wire. She left it to him. He bought the wire and soon laid £5 aside for fear he "get ketched". In a few years he had £40 of furniture in his house. He was only caught once.'

He was probably a Hampshire man, for Eleanor Eden was a Hampshire lady, but the trade flourished equally in our Wiltshire villages, for Winterslow had a celebrated coaching inn which was undoubtedly a much-used collecting-centre.

Now known as the Pheasant Inn, it is a well-known and

popular hostelry on the A30 highway, about seven miles east of Salisbury. Readers may recall that it featured in a series of four postage stamps issued to celebrate the centenary of the Royal Mail in 1988. The episode depicted is the somewhat bizarre one of stage-coach horses being attacked by a lioness in the inn courtyard.

On an October night in 1816, as the Exeter mail coach drew up, one of the leading horses was pounced on by a lioness which had escaped from a travelling menagerie. In the ensuing panic, the passengers tumbled out of the coach, scampered into the inn and barred the door – unfortunately leaving one of their number outside. The coachman and the guard remained on their seats, from which the guard tried to shoot the attacker with his blunderbuss. A Newfoundland dog grabbed the lioness by a leg but was forced to retire, considerably the worse for the encounter. Its intervention, however, distracted the lioness, which, alarmed by all the commotion, took refuge among the staddle stones supporting a granary nearby.

The menagerie proprietor and his assistants now came hurrying up. Having assessed the situation and being alarmed at the prospect of someone shooting such a valuable animal, the proprietor, with truly remarkable courage, started to crawl under the granary. There, by the light of candles, according to the *Salisbury & Winchester Journal*, they ' ... placed a sack on the ground near her and made her lie down upon it; they then tied her four legs and passed a cord around her mouth, which they secured; in this state they drew her out from under the granary, upon the sack, and then she was lifted and carried by six men into her den in the caravan'.

This lively incident had three major sequels. The unfortunate horse, whose name was Pomegranate, was exhibited, with all her wounds, by the menagerie-owner at Salisbury Fair next day. The passenger who, in the wild rush for the inn, had been left outside was banging at the door when the lioness, retreating from the dog, bumped into him. The experience proved too much for the poor man, who after a few days was admitted to Laverstock Asylum, where he spent the remaining twenty-seven years of his life. Finally the lioness story became a popular saga. No doubt it was told with relish by stage-coach passengers arriving in London during the next few weeks. Artists took it up and produced dozens of oil paintings of it, particularly painted trays. Some reproductions still adorn the walls of the Pheasant Inn. One, present whereabouts unknown to the author, depicts the lioness clawing at the horse, but the inn is not the Pheasant but the Clerkenwell Inn, at the London terminus of the stage-coach! The story was obviously too good to be wasted on a provincial hostelry! So Winterslow's lioness has taken her place in the folklore of England.

The Pheasant Inn lies in the trough between two long hills on a straight stretch of the A30. It was originally known as Winterslow Hut and was apparently a rough sort of hut, much used by drovers, on the opposite side of the road to the present Pheasant. The site was probably dictated by the presence of a spring in the adjacent pond, which offered the only water available for miles over the unfenced, uncultivated downs. At seven miles from Salisbury, it marked the ideal place for a change of horses when the era of the stage-coach began.

That is generally reckoned to be about 1750. The stage-coaches which operated a hundred years earlier were massive, cumbersome vehicles, without springs, lumbering at an infinitesimal pace over the unmade roads. One in 1658 advertised a service from London to Salisbury in two days, at the price of 20 shillings.

By the 1770s the fare from Salisbury to London was 8 or 10 shillings, and the journey occupied just a day. The transformation is explained by the improvement of the roads. Traditionally the upkeep of roads was the responsibility of the parish in which they were situated. The parish authorities naturally gave priority to roads linking them with their neighbours and the nearest market town. Long-distance traffic held little interest for them, nor was there much hope of inducing them to take a less parochial attitude.

Progress came by the introduction of the turnpike system, the essence of which was toll roads. Throughout the eighteenth century Parliament passed several hundred Road Acts enabling companies to take over a stretch of the highway and, in return for providing and maintaining it, to erect toll gates and make appropriate charges.

Much of the A30 quickly became a series of turnpikes. Under an overhanging chalk bank by St Thomas's Bridge, two miles out of Salisbury, a whitewashed, slate-roofed bungalow, demolished only a few years ago, had originally been built for the tollgate keeper. Here the turnpike ended, a cast-iron signpost marking the demarcation line between the turnpike and the 'County Bridge Road'. Similar tollgate houses in some numbers still survive in the countryside. Situated right on the roadside, they are usually octagonal or round, with windows commanding views in every direction. They were obviously designed to ensure that no one slipped by without paying a toll.

They were unpopular with country folk. Tolls were an innovation, and the associated improvement in the road surface meant little to them. An old farm account book gives a list of tolls: a penny for a horse; 4 pence for a horse and vehicle; 2 shillings for a wagon-load of corn drawn by four horses; cattle on the hoof, 10 pence per score animals; sheep 8 pence a score. This was at a time when the price of a sheep was 20 shillings, and beef sold at 5 pence a pound. The farmers considered they had grievances – and that was only the beginning of them.

Having taken his corn to market and sold it, a farmer would naturally load the wagon with something – perhaps coal or timber or oilseed cake – for the return journey. Thereupon the tollgate keeper charged him a further 2 shillings. And for a load weighing more than a ton, an excess charge was made. Who estimated the weight of the load? Why, the tollgate keeper, of course!

In general, turnpike roads serviced relatively short stretches, often only five or six miles. So farmers attending market from the more distant villages had to pay two lots of tolls to get to town. And two more on the way home. At the height of the system many market-towns were so fenced in by tollgates that it was impossible even to take a horse out for exercise without paying a toll.

One suspects, though, that Salisbury was not such a

town. The farmers of Pitton, Farley and Winterslow could, and undoubtedly did, get to market by following devious routes by lanes and farm tracks, probably involving the Clarendon Estate and the back entrance to the city by way of Milford. The turnpike that is now the A30 was not really intended to trap them but to supply the need for a long-distance route between London and the West.

Apparently the London–Salisbury road was taken over by turnpikes between 1750, when the system began to gather momentum, and 1837. Prior to 1750 the highway west from Basingstoke was 'a miserable waggon track, without a single turnpike'. No wonder the journey from London to Salisbury took two days. In 1837, however, Sir Richard Colt Hoare, the historian of Wiltshire, refers to the road as 'The London Turnpike', and further evidence of the improvement of the surface is provided by a contemporary comment, 'No horse walks a yard now between London and Exeter … all *Trotting Ground!*'

At the peak of the coaching era three coaches a day ran between Salisbury and London, in each direction. These were the *Sovereign*, the *Royal Mail* and the *Regulator*, all completing the journey in around twenty-two hours. In addition the Salisbury Diligence ran every night. Also frequenting the road were the huge hooded wagons which carried goods between Falmouth and London, needing twelve days for the journey. They were drawn by teams of eight heavy horses, with a maximum speed of three miles an hour, and that only when urged on by a man mounted on a pony and wielding a long whip. Travellers on foot could easily keep up with the wagons and often did so, their luggage stowed on the wagons with other cargo. When they stopped for the night at such an inn as the Pheasant, the travellers would try to persuade the innkeeper to allow them to sleep in a loft; otherwise they had to bed down under the wagons.

Through much of the stage-coach epoch the Salisbury–London road was infested by highwaymen, one of whom, Thomas Boulter, has a special connection with Winterslow Hut. It was there that he held up his first stage-coach, being, as he afterwards recorded in his reminiscences, so frightened that 'perspiration streamed from every pore' and he rode two or three times around the Diligence, the coach which he had marked as his prey, before he summoned up enough courage to cry, 'Stand and deliver!' Later he overcame his nervousness and carried out so many daring exploits that he was widely known as 'the Flying Highwayman'. At least some of the stories associated with Dick Turpin belong rightly to Thomas Boulter, who really did have a horse called Black Bess, which he had stolen from a stable in Erlestoke Park. In the end he was hanged at Winchester.

The stage-coaches, and indeed the episode of the lioness, must have been familiar to William Hazlitt, the essayist, who at that time was living at Winterslow. Mary Stodart, a great friend of Charles and Mary Lamb, had inherited a small house at Winterslow, and after his marriage to her in 1808 William Hazlitt went to live with her there, at a time when he was doing much of his best work. One of his essays, published posthumously under the title 'Winterslow Essay', was introduced by a preface by his son, who recalls, 'In olden times, when we lived in the village itself ... Charles and Mary Lamb would pay us frequent visits, rambling about all the time.' It is said that sometimes they would walk as much as forty miles a day. When, later, his marriage with Mary Stodart foundered, Hazlitt continued to visit Winterslow ('where most of his thinking was done', his son comments), making his base Winterslow Hut, where he slept in a great four-poster still available to visitors to the Pheasant. Charles Dickens and several friends, riding over Salisbury Plain in 1848 (eighteen years after Hazlitt's death), made a point of 'exploring Hazlitt's Hut'.

What a bustling place Winterslow Hut must have been in the heyday of the stage-coach! What activity when a coach was due! The inn lies in a bottom between two long, steep hills, and when the coaches came over the top of these hills the guards sounded their horns to give warning of their approach. That was the signal for the fresh horses, ready harnessed, to be led from their stables to replace the four who had been trotting for the past seven miles. Would-be passengers with their luggage would assemble in the courtyard, together with hampers, boxes and

cargoes of every description. The coaches ran to as strict a
time schedule as possible and must not be kept waiting.

If the three London-based coaches and the Salisbury
Diligence each had their complement of horses in
readiness at the Hut, there must always have been at least
sixteen excellent horses in the stables, and probably more,
for provision had to be made for sickness or casualties.
And they were only a proportion of the equine
population, for everyone (except the farm labourers, who
walked) coming to meet the coaches rode horse-back.
Besides which, there were those long-distance wagons,
with their heavy horses of Shire type, plodding along with
their enormous loads and requiring food and stabling for
the night.

Much of the land around the Hut was still open
downland, where a horseman might ride where he willed,
but several well-used lanes led to the villages of the forest
margins to the south. Two climbed the hill to Winterslow
village and linked up with other roads leading to
Tytherley, Farley and Dean. A third kept to the valley floor
and joined Pitton's Bottom Way. Tracks over the downs to
the north led to Porton, Idmiston, Winterbourne and the
other villages of the Bourne valley.

Winterslow Hut was thus a motorway service station of
the stage-coach age, though its importance was enhanced
by there being no alternative. Modern travellers can
choose to make their journeys by road, rail or plane, but
for those of the early Victorian age there was no such
choice. The turnpiked highway was the only route to
London. The Hut was the entrepôt for the entire district.
Not that the agricultural labourers who comprised the
greater part of the rural population had any direct
dealings with London, though even that was beginning to
change. Arthur Young, pioneer of agricultural authors,
writing in 1771 noted how things were shaping:

'But now! a country fellow, one hundred miles from
London, jumps on a coach box in the morning and, for
eight or ten shillings, gets to town by night, which makes
a material difference; besides rendering the going up and
down so easy, the numbers *who have seen London* are
increased tenfold, and of course ten times the boasts are

sounded in the ears of country fools to induce them to quit their healthy clean fields for a region of dirt, stink and noise.'

He was, of course, writing before the wholesale enclosures had done their evil work.

For those who could not or did not wish to travel to London, staging-posts such as the Winterslow Hut were nevertheless a highly valued link with the outside world. Even in the seventeenth century, when even the main highways were rough, muddy tracks, Sir Stephen Fox used to send over from Farley to collect his letters from the Winterslow Hut. Hazlitt, from his cottage in Winterslow, had to do the same – and once had occasion to complain to the Salisbury postmaster about the Winterslow Hut landlady's refusing to part with his letters when he sent a penny too little to pay for them! Doubtless she had had some experience of defaulting debtors.

It was no wonder that one of the first roads to be given a hard surface after the Pitton and Farley enclosures of 1810 was the Bottom Way northwards from Pitton. Previously traffic between Pitton and Winterslow used the direct route over the hill, now known as Winterslow Hollow; no one would have thought of taking the detour by way of Dunstable Corner. But the Bottom Way was important because it led direct to the Winterslow Hut!

The attractions of the Hut are not difficult to appreciate when we recall that, as in an instance already quoted, some villagers lived out their lives without ever venturing more than two or three miles from their birthplace. Fancy being able to trudge along the Bottom Way to the Hut and see a real live lioness and all the other animals of a travelling menagerie! And to see stage-coaches *en route* to or from London pull up several times a day! To say nothing of the great cargo wagons from distant Devon and Cornwall, and the still numerous droves of sheep and cattle under the charge of drovers making their way on the hoof to distant markets! And the opportunity to exchange gossip and news not only with the travellers but with men from the neighbouring villages on errands for their employers.

A visit to the Hut was a social occasion, an aspect of the

situation which the proprietors catered for. Compiling the Winterslow Women's Institute Scrapbook in the 1920s, the editors record that one of the members remembered her father 'dancing his shoes to pieces' at the Hut, during 'the week of the Hutt Revels'. They also noted that, 'At the other side of the house is a large empty room, formerly devoted to cock fighting matches and single stick combats.' In the author's possession is an example of the single sticks used in these contests.

The stage-coach era came to an abrupt end, as far as Winterslow Hut was concerned, in the 1840s, when the railway reached Salisbury. In 1850 a contemporary writer described the Hut as ' ... a desolate place ... a small farm of 30 acres – in winter two or three weeks pass without even a beggar or tramp passing the door ...'. This, however, may have been an unduly pessimistic comment, for in the 1870s it still evidently had a fairly flourishing life of its own. The 'Hutt Revels' were still held, and it seems that the Winterslow Mummers still met there. Sportsmen, interested in shooting or coursing the wildlife of the Plain (including bustards), came to stay for a night or two.

The author's great-uncle, Arthur Whitlock, a notorious – or celebrated – poacher in his day, was evidently a frequent visitor to the Pheasant, as it had now become, in the 1890s. One afternoon the landlord beckoned him outside from the public bar.

'I got two gents from London in there,' indicating the inn parlour. 'Got a greyhound they wants to try out on a hare. Know where to find one?'

'Can't say that I do,' said Arthur. 'Not a live one. I got a *dead* un in me bag ... Wait a bit, though. Wait a bit. Tell em to hang on for ten minutes and I'll see what I can do.'

Out in the courtyard he deftly skinned his hare. Using a morsel of fresh meat as bait, he grabbed one of the inn cats – a numerous tribe – and wrapped her in it, fastening it on as tightly as he could. He pushed the scared cat into his bag and called through the window to the innkeeper.

'You can tell they gents to bring their dog out here. I be ready for 'em.'

'I got a hare in this yer bag,' he explained to the sportsmen, when they emerged. 'Now, I wants for you to stand just here with yer dog. Keep a tight leash on en till I gives the word, and then let en go, quick.'

'I'd better have my two guineas off ee now,' he added, 'cos I got to get on. I be late for work as it is.'

So the money changed hands, Arthur up-ended the bag, and the sportsmen released their greyhound. Of course, the cat shot across the yard and up the nearest tree, before the hound could catch her. When the men had retrieved it, barking, from the foot of the tree, and looked round to see where Arthur was, he had disappeared.

'I thought I'd better get on,' he used to explain, when telling the tale. 'It was true what I said, about being late for work.' Then he would add, 'I'd have given a lot to have heard they two Londoners telling their posh city friends how down in Wiltshire they'd seen hares what climbed trees!'

Although the incident happened late in the century, when poaching was not such a dire offence as it had been fifty years earlier, it is interesting that the Pheasant still had a reputation as an inn associated with poachers. The tradition survived from the days when it was a collecting-depot for game from all over the district. Examination of the crates, barrels, portmanteaus, hampers, kitbags, boxes and other containers carried on the luggage racks and roofs of the stage-coaches would have revealed, under layers of innocent commodities, vast quantities of closely packed pheasants, partridges, hares and other game, as well as fresh eggs of game-birds in the proper season.

The clandestine trade did not lack organization. It was not a matter of a casual poacher trudging along to Winterslow Hut after dark and surreptitiously handing a couple of pheasants to one of the stable-hands, though doubtless that did happen. Nor were 'higglers' – dealers who dealt in anything, including game, on a small scale and were often gypsies or didicois – its chief agents. But in every village there existed depots – sometimes cottages but more often barns, sheds or perhaps the village smithy – where game could be concealed until transport was available to take it to the rendezvous with the stage-coach. At the Hut, more concealment in sheds, cellars, perhaps even in the granary under which the lioness took refuge, until the dangerous contraband could be safely transferred to vehicles bound for London. The Salisbury coaches were among the 300 which daily passed Hyde Park Corner in 1824, and it seems to have been widely known that in the weeks before Christmas many of them carried a greater weight in dead passengers than in living ones.

In London there was no lack of customers. In addition to the clubs and hotels, butchers and poulterers offered an insatiable market. A London dealer told a select committee on the game laws that he did business with 19,000 suppliers of game, most of them unregistered. Mrs Beeton, whose first cookery book was published in 1859/60, included in it more than forty recipes for game, commenting, 'There are innumerable Acts of Parliament inflicting penalties on persons who illegally kill game, and some of them are very severe; but they cannot be said to answer their end, nor can it be expected that they ever will, whilst there are so many persons of great wealth who have not otherwise means of procuring game except by purchase, and who *will have it.*'

Such a vast and lucrative market could not possibly be supplied from legitimate sources, and so the black market flourished. Rural poachers poached to order, knowing exactly how many birds they needed to take for their next consignment. A further complication was introduced by gamekeepers joining in the traffic. Many of the 100,000 pheasant and partridge eggs which appeared illicitly every year on the London market, according to the testimony of another witness before the select committee on the game laws, must have been supplied from this source.

The poachers of Pitton and Farley (alias the greater part of the population) possessed one notable advantage when engaging in this traffic. Their absentee landlord, the Earl of Ilchester, was a strict game-preserver, valuing his estates as much for the sport they afforded him on his occasional visit as for the rents. The harsh old rule that a man could be evicted from his farm or cottage if convicted of poaching still applied. But just over the fence, within a stone's throw of the nearest Pitton cottages, was Lord Bathurst's Clarendon Estate, where such a sanction could not apply. Pitton and Farley men helped themselves unceasingly to Sir Frederick's pheasants and partridges, despite all the efforts of his keepers. The guerrilla war went on through most of the century, with advantages sometimes to one side, sometimes to the other. Fines were no real deterrent, when farm wages were 7 to 9 shillings a week and the price of a cock pheasant half-a-guinea. Even a few weeks in Fisherton Gaol could be faced with some equanimity.

A perusal of some of the petty sessions records for Salisbury and Amesbury in the mid-nineteenth century briefly illuminate the lives of some of the poachers of Pitton and Farley.

George Whitlock, of Pitton, features quite frequently. On 24 January 1843, at the Council House, Salisbury, he is ' ... convicted of trespassing in pursuit of Game at Clarendon Park on the 16th of January instant on the land of Sir Frederick Bathurst. Fined £1.5s.10d and costs. In default of payment to be imprisoned in the house of correction at Fisherton Anger for six weeks.' His next appearance before the magistrates was on 12 December 1848, when he was ' ... convicted of using a gun to kill game at Pitton and Farley on the 4th December inst. Fined £5 and costs. In default to be imprisoned at the House of Correction at Fisherton Anger for three calendar months.' Three years later, on 20 May 1851, his conviction is for ' ... knowingly having in his possession and control eight pheasant's eggs, at the parish of Pitton and Farley, on the 18th day of May instant. Fined 5s for each egg, together 40s. In default of payment to be imprisoned in the House of Correction at Fisherton Anger for one calendar month.'

Probably he paid the fines, for three convictions in eight years would have seemed to George a reasonable outlay. He doubtless considered himself well ahead of the game.

A somewhat sinister and unpleasant element enters the chronicles anent George's offences. Appended to the entry of 24 January 1843 is a receipt for 12s.9d., 'the moiety of fine imposed on George Whitlock. Signed ... Richard M ......, informer'. Again, on 6 June 1851, ' ... one pound moiety of penalty imposed on the above-named George Whitlock, Signed, Richard Jenkins, informer'.

It is possible, of course, that the informers in these instances were gamekeepers employed by Sir Frederick Bathurst, in which case they were simply doing their job. The presence of informers in the countryside, no matter what their credentials, must have been a cause of friction between neighbours. Ted Whitlock once witnessed a bitter exchange of oaths and insults when his Uncle Arthur passed a keeper in the village street.

An inspection of the 1851 census for Pitton reveals a few facts about George Whitlock. Or rather, it would if there had not been two George Whitlocks living in Pitton at that time. One is a woodman aged fifty, living in a cottage by Pitton Green, with his son James, aged nineteen and his daughter Ellen, aged fifteen. He is stated to be married, though no wife is mentioned. The other is George Whitlock, agricultural labourer, aged thirty-seven, widower living with his son Job, aged eight. This second George is almost certainly our poacher. The first George, being a woodman, would not have risked being banned from the Bathurst estate, where most of his work probably lay.

Incidentally, the Salisbury petty sessions records for the 1850s supply other evidence of disharmony among villagers. On 2 November 1855 William Whitlock, yeoman, of Winterslow, prosecutes Mary Ann Young and Stephen Judd for ' ... stealing one weight of bacon on 1st inst, the property of the prosecutor, and the said Stephen Judd for receiving the same. Sentence, each to be imprisoned in the House of Correction at Fisherton Anger for three days. Total amount of expenses £1.13s.6d. Justice clerk's fees, 16s.6d.'

This William Whitlock was then aged twenty-seven, farming New Manor Farm (625 acres) and employing fifteen men. The case looks like the hasty reaction of a young man catching pilferers red-handed, for the offence took place on 1 November and the culprits were hauled before the magistrates the next day.

The incident evidently rankled, but revenge had to be postponed till 4 November 1856. On that date William Whitlock, yeoman, of Winterslow, is in the dock, accused of 'trespassing on land in the occupation of Samuel

Lampard in search and pursuit of Game at Pitton and Farley on October 22nd last'. The hearing was twice adjourned, in view of the status of the defendant, but was at last taken on 18 November, when William was ' ... convicted in the penalty of 10s. and costs. In default of payment to be imprisoned in the House of Correction at Fisherton Anger for 14 days.' Then, finally, that revealing postscript: ' ... received, January 7th, 1858, five shillings moiety of penalty imposed on William Whitlock, signed, Arthur Messill, informer'.

The obvious reconstruction is that Mary Ann Young and Stephen Judd, smarting under the fine imposed and even more at being caught, enlisted the aid of their friends and relations (doubtless half the inhabitants of Winterslow) to catch out William in some indictable offence. They had to wait for a year, and then the unwary William, walking the fields of his own farm, crossed the boundary into that of his neighbour, Samuel Lampard. Perhaps he had shot a partridge and gone to retrieve it. Anyway, it was sufficient. Mary Ann and Stephen had their revenge, and the alert Arthur Messill collected his reward.

William Whitlock appears to have mellowed in his later years and to have achieved a reputation for philanthropy, for towards the end of the century Winterslow paupers claimed that they ' ... were clothed quite well, thank you, out of Willie Whitlock's rag-bag'.

As a footnote to this chapter, the Salisbury petty sessions minute book contains a very curious paragraph:

December 5th, 1853
James Whitlock, of Pitton, labourer, convicted of being the driver but not the owner of a Waggon and two horses proceeding on the Turnpike Road at Milford on the first of December instant ... and thereon having no other person to guide the horses. Fined £1 and costs. In default of payment to be imprisoned in the House of Correction at Fisherton Anger for 21 days. Paid.

What on earth was this offence which earned a heavier penalty than poaching? Evidently it had something to do with the turnpike regulations, but why should a wagon

A Victorian Village

and two horses need the services of two men? Probably the owner of the vehicle and therefore the employer of James Whitlock paid the fine, muttering curses against bureaucracy, of which this seems to be a classic example. Or is there some other explanation?

12   The Shadow of the Workhouse

After the turbulence of the early decades of the nineteenth century, the middle years were a period of quiet and steadily increasing prosperity. Action had tended to retreat from the countryside and centre on the mush-rooming industrial towns. Becoming increasingly conscious of its own numerical and economic strength, the urban populace agitated and at times rioted until at length they managed to force through Parliament a series of Reform Bills, which eventually produced a universal franchise and imposed considerable restraints on, even if it did not entirely abolish, the dominance of the country gentry.

One of the early acts of the reforming Parliaments was to repeal (in 1846) the Corn Laws, which had kept the price of food unduly high. Contrary to much gloomy foreboding, this measure did not spell immediate ruin for the countryside. Instead, farming England settled down to a period of peaceful prosperity and progress.

In 1803 Thomas Malthus published his great work promulgating the theory that populations inevitably outgrow their food supply and are kept in check by natural hardships and disasters. In the century which followed there seemed every likelihood that he would be proved correct, as far as England was concerned. The population exploded from about 11 millions at the beginning of the century to over 40 millions at the end, most of the increase being in the still expanding industrial towns.

Here was the background to the era of Victorian high farming – the Golden Age of Agriculture. By investing in the new types of machinery turned out by town factories, by the scientific breeding of livestock, by crop-improvement and by reclaiming many thousands of acres of formerly waste land, English farmers just about managed to keep pace with the needs of the urban population.

The resultant prosperity affected most country-dwellers. Far from experiencing the decline they had feared, the great agricultural estates flourished as never before. Yeomen farmers accumulated fortunes. Working farmers at a lower level improved their standard of living; their wives insisted on setting aside a front room as a drawing-room, equipped with a new piano. Even the labourers fared better than before. They could look back on the 'hungry forties' as 'the bad old days' and forget about the even worse times of the thirties.

The population of Pitton at that time consisted preponderantly of agricultural labourers but had a fair leavening of other occupants. According to the 1851 census, there were six farmers, plus one retired, and 102 agricultural labourers – though incidentally many of these were boys in their early teens. Elisha Whitlock, with his five acres, is in an anomalous category, as 'farmer and woodman'. Woodmen proper, including men classified as 'labourers in the woods', total nine. There are also one hurdle-maker and one brush-maker.

One of the most interesting features, however, is the development of ancillary industries. The village now has two flourishing building firms, the Pitts and the Brieants. Between them they employ seven journeyman carpenters, two master carpenters, three turners, one master bricklayer, one ordinary bricklayer and one journeyman bricklayer, one journeyman blacksmith and two sawyers: eighteen skilled workers in all. A useful leavening in an otherwise agricultural community. Incidentally, much of the work done in the builders' yards was intimately associated with farming. The Pitts were celebrated wagon-builders. Around this time, too, the Brieants established a lime-burning industry by White Hill.

The village had two shoemakers and a cordwainer – a distinction now obsolete. Stephen Offer kept the New Inn and employed one barmaid. The four housekeepers presumably kept house for the larger farmers, who also doubtless employed the two servants listed. The Church of England primary school, established in 1850, had thirty scholars, under the tuition of two schoolmistresses. Of the two men classified as pensioners, one was a one-legged ex-soldier. In all, a reasonably well balanced rural community.

Things continued to improve through the 1850s and were even better in the 1860s. The 1870s were better still – until 1875. Then disaster struck.

The emigration policy fostered earlier in the century by the country landowners and larger farmers now brought its own nemesis. Endless shiploads of grain began to pour in from the prairies of the United States and Canada, to be followed soon afterwards by endless cargoes of refrigerated meat from Australia, New Zealand and South Africa. The descendants of the former peasants who had been driven overseas were now producing a surplus of food which threatened the stability of the home market. The descendants of the former peasants who had been driven from their homes into the industrial towns were now completely out of sympathy with country life. The emigrants made available supplies of cheap food – far cheaper than it could be produced on English farms; the urban voters made sure that no protective legislation should keep them out.

English farmers, continuing to farm in the manner which had served them so well for several decades, could not understand what had gone wrong. The well-established and basically sound system of sheep-and-corn farming, so admirably suited to chalk soils, was particularly vulnerable. Bankruptcies among sheep farmers were particularly high.

Between 1875 and 1895 agriculture floundered in a

morass. The corn acreage declined by some twenty-five per cent; prices of home-produced food were nearly halved; farm rents fell by more than twenty per cent; more than twenty-five per cent of agricultural workers left the land for other jobs. Royal commissions in 1879 and 1893 took due note of the agricultural depression but could do little to alleviate it.

We now arrive at a point at which it is possible to invest more of the dry statistics of names in parish registers and censuses with some sort of life. For the final quarter of the nineteenth century we have the benefit of a contemporary document set in our Victorian village. It consists of the reminiscences of Ted Whitlock, as related to his son, the author of this book, on winter evenings in the 1930s.

Let us see where Ted, who was born in 1874, fits into the pattern of events.

We know that he was the son of Daniel Whitlock, who married Jane Noyce of Winterslow in 1868 or 1869. And Daniel we can find, as a boy of nine, in the 1851 census. His father was William Whitlock, whom Ted could remember as an old man known in the village as 'Donkey Bill'. Of Daniel he knew little, except that he died in tragic and somewhat mysterious circumstances when the boy was six months old. Ted's mother, Jane, once told him that she had '... prayed about his father and believed that he had gone to Heaven, after all', which suggested to Ted that there was some doubt about the matter. When he asked his uncles about it, however, they refused to tell him anything, saying, 'You must ask your mother.'

In 1851 there were three William Whitlocks in Pitton and one in Winterslow. The Winterslow William was, of course, the proprietor of New Manor Farm, whom we have already met. Naturally he was related to all the other Whitlocks in the district, though the ramifications are almost impossible to unravel.

The William Whitlocks of Pitton are:

1. William Whitlock, aged forty-six, living with his wife Ann and two children, Uriah, aged seven, and Sarah, aged two. He is described as an agricultural labourer and pensioner. Ted knew him as a one-legged ex-soldier

known locally as 'Sergeant Whitlock'. His family was not complete in 1851, for later Mary-Ann and Walter were born. Uriah became the village shopkeeper and baker, and the whole family played a prominent part in village life during much of Ted's lifetime.

2. William Whitlock, aged thirty-nine, living with his wife Sarah and five children, aged from thirteen to one. He too was an agricultural labourer. Only one of the children was a boy, Job, and neither he nor his father feature in Ted's memoirs. Perhaps they moved away from Pitton.

3. William Whitlock, aged thirty-five, a widower living with his three children, Daniel, aged nine, Phillida (here spelt 'Felida'), aged five, and Susannah, aged three. This is, of course, our William Whitlock. He is described as an agricultural labourer and has an unmarried niece keeping house for him.

One other Whitlock household has a close relevance to our story. It is that of Charles Whitlock, aged twenty-seven, an agricultural labourer living with his wife Charlotte, aged twenty-eight, and their son Arthur, aged seven months.

William and Charles were brothers, and Arthur features prominently in Ted's memoirs as an uncle who did what he could to help the orphaned lad in his early years. Arthur ought to have been christened Charles, the villagers maintained, for his name broke a sequence of five generations of eldest sons named Charles – an item of gossip which has proved useful to subsequent researchers into family history.

We have noted two George Whitlocks and now three William Whitlocks; there were in addition two Charles Whitlocks, two Thomas Whites, two John Whites, two Samuel Collinses, two William Collinses and two George Collinses, all heads of households, to say nothing of sundry small fry. With so many villagers bearing the same name, it was obviously necessary to devise some method of distinguishing between them. The Welsh method of referring to 'Jones the Post' or 'Evans the Shop' could not be applied, for virtually all of them were simply farm labourers. Nicknames were one solution. 'Donkey Bill' (because William Whitlock possessed a donkey) and 'Sergeant Whitlock', the ex-soldier, were examples. A common device, however, was to refer to men by their mother's surnames. Thus Charles Whitlock whom we have noted as a young man, the father of Arthur, later became the father of two more boys, Jesse and Joseph. Now Charles was married to a Charlotte whose maiden name was Pearce; and his father, another Charles, had been married to a lady whose maiden name was Head. So the three brothers were familiarly known as Arth Pearce, Jesse Head and Joe Whitlock!

Most of these farm workers of the mid-century, and the Whitlocks in particular, were short, stocky men. Ted, of the next generation, was not much above five feet in height, though with a strong, sturdy frame. Time and again in his reminiscences he refers to so-and-so's being 'a little man'. So Arthur, who was above average height as well as being well built, was conspicuous among his contemporaries. He also had qualities of leadership, an air of confidence and a devil-may-care attitude which led him into lots of scrapes. It was widely whispered that he was not Charles's son, but such complications were by no means unknown in our villages and were absorbed without fuss.

The women were even smaller of stature than the men. Exhibitions of early nineteenth-century dresses, which usually feature mostly wedding dresses, depict most women as less than five feet tall – tiny things, with slender waists and dainty fingers.

Daniel's bride, Jane Noyce, worked in London as a domestic servant (in some comparatively exalted position such as parlour-maid) before her marriage. As a wedding present the ladies who employed her sewed an exquisitely executed christening gown for the babies which she would inevitably produce. Jane's three children were, in fact, christened in it, and so were Ted's three. It is now a treasured family heirloom, at present in the author's possession. But when the author's family arrived, only the first, weighing 6½ pounds, was small enough to get into it! The other two, at 7½ and nine pounds were far too big and plump! Their mother had to sew another christening gown for them. The inference is that not only were the early nineteenth-century women small and dainty, but so were the babies.

Let us now see what information Ted can give us in his memoirs of the characters with whom he shared his early life in Pitton.

Donkey Bill
This was William Whitlock, Ted's grandfather. In 1851 he is recorded as a widower with three small children. Later he married again, reputedly to a school-teacher named Elizabeth. A school-teacher named Elizabeth is indeed mentioned in the 1851 census, but she is married to one John Williams. She is, in any case, aged forty-three, so as William's second wife bore him several children, it could hardly have been this Elizabeth, even if she had been widowed soon afterwards. William must have met his new bride elsewhere.

There are hints of some friction between the two families, and an allegation that Jane, Daniel's widow, had to resort to law to retain possession of her cottage, coveted by Elizabeth. In later years, however, Ted's relationship with his step-uncles was perfectly amicable.

Ted remembers his grandfather, Donkey Bill, as 'a skinny little old man with a slightly hooked nose and a thin beard'. When his second family was small, he was kicked by a horse. The leg was badly set and neglected, with the result that he was never again able to take a regular job on the farm. Of course, he received no compensation, and while he was in bed the whole family had to 'go on the parish'.

He managed for a time on casual work, such as hoeing, haymaking and harvesting, but when he grew too old to earn much that way he started a business of his own. At the age of seventy he bought a cheap handcart and hobbled around the villages collecting wood ashes from the householders and selling them as manure to the farmers. Everybody burned only wood then, and there were quantities of ashes to be obtained from most households, for most of them baked bread.

By now released from the burden of raising a family, William throve modestly in his new business. After a few years he was able to buy a donkey to pull the cart, and so acquired his nickname. When Ted was a boy, old Donkey Bill and his donkey were among the features of Pitton. The donkey herself was a character, liable to lash out without warning at anyone who approached her. She may have had reason for such behaviour, for boys were not above sticking a pin into her rump if they got the chance.

At the far end of the village stood an ancient elm of immense girth and hollow with age. Its top had been blown off in an autumn gale, and its scarred, rugged stump stood like a stark sentinel guarding the Winterslow road. Farmer Seaward permitted Donkey Bill to use the hollow bole for storing his ashes. Ted recalled:

> One Sunday morning the elm caught fire. Flames shot out from the entrance, and the smoke found a dozen outlets among the twigs and brushwood. The villagers assembled with buckets of water and good advice. Donkey Bill hopped about among them in an agony of concern, and it was no thanks to him that the fire was eventually put out. For us boys it was a glorious excuse for missing Sunday School and morning service at chapel. For punishment I was made to attend the evening service, and by coincidence the sermon was on the subject of Moses and the burning bush! ...
>
> Towards the end of his life William lived in a minute two-roomed cottage attached to Box Cottage. In later years the Collins boys used it as a bicycle shed. The entire building was no larger than a normal-sized room, with a partition across the middle to make one bedroom and one living-room. William and Elizabeth were quite comfortable there, for their needs were few. They were better off than the previous occupants, the Jerreds. Thomas Jerred was a married man with five children.
>
> At the far end of the garden was the inevitable outdoor lavatory – a conspicuous, tiled, sentry-box of a shed. Here on a June afternoon Donkey Bill was found dead upon the seat. Outside stood the donkey, harnessed to the cart and waiting for the old man to come and finish the day's work.
>
> We avoided a pauper's funeral. Elizabeth made a fuss and seemed cut up, but whether that was because she was genuinely fond of the old man (though she used to bully him

unmercifully) or whether it was because she knew it meant the workhouse for her is hard to say. She died in the workhouse two years later and is buried in Pitton churchyard in the same grave as William, though no one knows where that is, for it was never marked.

The Workhouse Bread-van

Ted could indulge in no reminiscences of his father, Daniel, for he had died when the boy was six months old. Nor could he glean much information from anyone he questioned, for there seemed to be a conspiracy of silence. 'You'll have to ask your mother,' was the standard reply. And Mother was saying nothing. Ted gathered that his father, at one time a regular attendant at chapel, had somehow fallen from grace and while in that state had unfortunately died, perhaps without repenting. But the details were withheld from him. He never knew what really happened, and the truth was revealed to his son, the author, only after Ted's death, as is related in our last chapter.

Of those bleak days following his father's sudden death Ted writes:

The one star in my mother's midnight was that she had a cottage to live in. It was her own. Daniel's grandfather Collins had built it in his spare time of chalk mud and flints on a tight little plot of land by White Hill. Only a cramped, moss-thatched building it was, with one room downstairs, a woodhouse and two little bedrooms, but it had been left in great-grandfather's will to his daughter 'Ann and her heirs for ever'. My father had inherited it. No one could turn my mother out.

When my mother applied to the guardians of the poor for parish relief, she had to tell them of the cottage and so, by the rules of the time, avoided being sent to the dreaded workhouse. The guardians of the poor duly considered her application and, finding no loophole for evasion, magnanimously decided to do their duty. They granted her 5 shillings a week and two loaves of workhouse bread. Then, as a rider, they added that of course she must do no charring or other domestic work for payment; it would never do to have paupers making money out of the rates.

Every Friday afternoon our dole arrived by the workhouse

bread-van. This was about the slowest vehicle I have ever seen, not excepting my grandfather's donkey cart. The horse was a real sleep-walker. It just staggered along, every rib as prominent as a newly struck furrow, till it reached the familiar destination, Donkey Bill's cottage. Taking the last few paces with a faltering effort, it stopped dead at finding the reins relax and immediately relapsed into a profound slumber. The poor animal was, of course, only half-alive, being dependent, like us, on the guardians of the poor for its livelihood. After all, if a woman and three small children were expected to live on 5 shillings a week and two loaves of bread, what could a horse expect?

On the front seat of the van the relieving officer and the driver sat bolt upright. They adopted this stiff attitude not so much to maintain their dignity as because a wooden partition rising vertically behind them made any other posture impossible.

The paupers, who had been gossiping, fell silent as the relieving officer descended. It took a little time, not only because he had a wooden leg but because a vigorous massage of thighs and bottom was necessary to disperse the inevitable pins-and-needles. When the blood began to circulate again, he glared or beamed upon the company (according to his mood and the state of the weather) and grumbled a few 'How-dee-dos'. The relieving officer was not an unkindly old man, though hard work and a long and intimate acquaintance with the seamier side of life had roughened him. He was paid by the guardians of the poor.

He climbed the steps to the cottage and seated himself in the chair placed for him on the far side of the table, dropping his jingling money-bag of faded chamois leather in front of him. A large red handkerchief appeared from a pocket and removed from his brow the perspiration or rain-drops or icicles that reflected the season of the year. Another pause. Then, after much fumbling in inner recesses, the tattered account-book and the iron-rimmed spectacles were produced, and business began.

Marking the lines with a thick forefinger, the relieving officer read out the names from his list, peering over his spectacles after each item. The women came forward one by one, friends appearing for those who were sick or bedridden. It was a lengthy procedure, for the relieving officer wanted to hear all the village news.

'Well, Mrs Sinnett, how're the chilblains?'

'Improvin', thank ee, Mr Butt; improvin' they be. I bin

rubbin' em well be holly-berry ashes, and that do do em a power of good.'

'And how's the old man?'

'Oh, he just lies there, lookin' at the bedroom ceilin'. Bin there since last barley harvest, er have, an' cain't move 'ees left arm, neet 'ees left leg. Has to wait on en hand an' foot, like a baby, I do. Er's martle tryin' at times, too, cos er've never bin used to bidin' indoors, havin' alwis worked in the woods. Er cain't spell out words, sno, so there er got to lie be nowt to do but gaze at the ceilin'.'

'Ah, tis bad when they come to it, Mrs Sinnett. Tis bad for em. Anything in my line next door?'

'No, not yet, Mr Butt. Though twill happen 'fore you do come next, I 'llow.'

The relieving officer was also registrar of births and deaths.

The roll-call ended, the paupers flocked out to the bread-van where the driver, a workhouse inmate, was throwing open the back doors. Even a blind man would have known that the driver's hands were not clean. They were, however, as well acquainted with soap and water as were those of the other paupers who mixed the dough. A little extra grime on the surface was only in keeping with the unspeakable interior of the loaves.

The ingredients of workhouse bread were a perpetual mystery. Probably it contained some cheap flour (though this was doubted by some) and a proportion of mashed potatoes. We used to speculate on sawdust and sour milk, on bran and miller's offal. Sometimes we discovered sacking fibre, scraps of paper and bits of cockroaches, even mouse dung. The loaves were flat and never properly baked. Their flavour was sour and nauseous. Above all, they stank, with a peculiar, penetrating persistence.

Hungry as we were, we seldom finished our weekly allowance of workhouse bread. With half-empty stomachs we children sat around the table, eyeing a loaf wistfully, and finally slipped down from our perches with a blasphemous 'Thank God for a good tea, Amen', rather than touch the disgusting stuff. Grandma Noyce baked regularly once a fortnight and regularly sent down from Winterslow a quartern loaf, which tasted like honey to us ...

Gleaning

At chapel services Bible readings from the Book of Ruth meant more to Ted than they could to any present-day listener. He remembered:

My first recollection of anything to do with farming was going gleaning. When the crops were mown by scythe, there was plenty of work for women and girls to do in the harvest fields, but when the carting of the sheaves began, their chores ended for most of them, and they were allowed to go gleaning. My mother and my two sisters, Clara and Kate, and I went gleaning, too.

The chief equipment of a gleaner or 'leazer' was a 'lap-bag' of coarse sacking. This hung from the gleaner's waist, like an apron, and was the receptacle for loose ears of corn that had been broken from their stalks. Each gleaner followed the line of a rank of 'hiles' (stooks of sheaves), where, naturally there was more spilt corn than in the intervening spaces. The expert gleaner gathered the scattered straw with her right hand and passed them over to her left, until she had as many as she could carry. Then she twisted the bundle into a curious little knot and placed it beside her dinner basket. When the lap-bag was full, the ears were poured into a little sack brought for that purpose.

Gleaners began work about eight o'clock in the morning and continued until the evening light faded. They then carried home the booty from their day's labour. The mother took the heavy sack of corn, the children brought the bundles. Sometimes, when the leazing had been very good, it was necessary to make two journeys. Gleaning was a tiring task, back-aching, and so when we had been working all day in a field a mile from home we did not appreciate having to go back for a second load after the moon had risen.

There were no horse-rakes to clean the fields after harvest, and poultry for the most part lived in the farmyard all the year round, so a fair quantity of gleanings was usually left for 'the stranger and the widow and the fatherless', as in the Mosaic law. No farmer would dream of turning away the gleaners from his fields. There was, however, an unwritten rule that gleaners might not enter a field until every sheaf had been taken to the rick. Any gleaner who disregarded this tradition was told to get out and probably found it difficult to gain admission at the proper time. I have seen women turned out of a field when only half a load of sheaves remained to be carted. The wives of carters and shepherds were exempted from this rule and could glean as soon as a reasonable space was cleared.

Only wheat was gleaned. Sheep were fed on oat-stubbles,

and pigs on barley. A common sight in summer was a boy driving four or five sows and about forty piglets along a dusty road to the barleyfields. This wasn't such a difficult job as might be imagined, as once a sow had 'been stubblin'' she knew exactly what was afoot and caused no trouble.

It was strange how news that a wheatfield was vacant for gleaning travelled. Often when a score of gleaners were working in a field that had been leazed fairly clean, first one and then another disappeared, and presently it was whispered that Farmer Cook had cleared a field a mile away. Within minutes our field was empty and we were all hurrying to the new ground.

We couldn't afford to waste time. The corn wouldn't wait for us. I remember when a woman who had been gleaning with us stayed at home for a day and came the next day to the fields with a new baby, which she placed beside her dinner-basket. Nobody took much notice, except to admire the baby. It seemed a commonplace event.

The quantity of corn gleaned in a season by our household varied from two to six bushels. After harvest we cut off the straw three inches from the ear and sold it to a cottager who kept pigs. The ears were stored in sacks in our bedroom and occupied about half the room, leaving a narrow access space on one side of the bed. Sometimes we lay awake at night and listened to the mice scurrying and scampering beneath the sacks.

The corn was threshed with flails in a farmer's barn, and the chaff was left behind to pay for the use of the building. Labourers threshed their family's gleanings by lantern light on a winter evening. Uncle Arthur usually threshed ours.

When the miller from Winterbourne paid his weekly visit to Pitton, with flour for the shop, he took back with him for grinding any gleanings that had been threshed. The following week he brought back the flour but kept the bran and milling offal to pay for his work. If a cottager kept pigs and claimed all the coarser meals, he had to pay the miller a small fee.

At first I think my mother used to sell some of our flour for ready cash, but she kept back all she could, to be sent to Grandma Noyce's or Aunt Martha's for baking. Later we moved to a cottage with a bread-oven, so Mother could then bake her own bread.

The bread-oven was a long, coffin-shaped orifice in the side of the chimney, about four feet above the hearth. In our cottage it was so completely hidden behind cupboard and mantelpiece that no one who didn't know where to look would ever find it. On baking days it was filled with burning faggot-wood and left to heat for about half an hour until a certain stone or brick, called 'the firestone', at the back of the cavity glowed white-hot. Then the embers were scraped out and the kneaded dough was placed in position.

The loaves were as sweet and fresh a fortnight after baking as they were on the day they came out of the oven. Indeed, the economical housewife never put them before the family until they were three or four days old: they were so appetizing that the men ate too much. The bread was stored in a kind of net or frame called a 'kivver', which hung from the kitchen ceiling.

The one handicap bedevilling our cottage bakeries was 'rimy bread'. This seems to have been a kind of fungus or mildew, which attacked the interior of the loaves. When cut they appeared furry or cobwebby, like the rime of hoar frost on spiders' webs on a misty morning. It matured after the bread had been stored for a couple of days, and if it appeared in an oven in spring it affected every batch of bread throughout the summer. We knew of no cure, no preventative. The taste was vile, but we often had to eat it or go without bread ...

The other mainstay of cottage diet was cheese – sometimes of indifferent quality – concerning which Ted was familiar with the following rhyme:

Tis bread-and-cheese for breakfast;
And bread-and-cheese for lunch;
If we gets hungry in the day
Tis bread-and-cheese to munch;
After bread-and-cheese for nammit   (a midday snack)
Tis bread-and-cheese for tea,
And then again at supper-time –
That's what gets over me!

However, apart from the occasional products of Uncle Arthur's poaching forays, various other titbits came Jane's way. Ted used quite often to be sent down to Farmer Goulding's house (Jane used to call his wife 'Aunt Miriam', so there must have been some relationship) for butter or milk, and at pig-killing time in November chitterlings, scraps, faggots and other delicacies were freely available.

13   Ted at School

The Church of England school at Pitton was opened in 1850 and has given splendid service to the village for the past 140 years, a service which is still happily continuing. Before that there were two day schools in the village, one catering for fifteen girls and the other for fourteen boys and girls. The parents paid for five of these pupils, the expense of the other twenty-four being borne by the vicar. There was also a Sunday School, supported by voluntary subscription, which was attended by forty-eight girls.

Farley had a day school endowed by the first warden of Fox's Hospital (the Wardenry), which in 1830 had fifty-four pupils (thirty-three boys and twenty-one girls). A house and garden were provided for the schoolmaster, then a Mr Charles Smith, who had his son, aged seventeen, assisting him as an apprentice. It catered for Pitton as well as Farley, for it is on record that ten boys and ten girls from the two villages received free education. Parents paid a penny a week for each of the others, though the vicar helped with some of the poorer families. In 1828 a Sunday School, supported by public subscription, was started and in 1830 was attended by thirty-five boys and twenty-five girls.

In addition, there are memories of comparatively short-lived dames' schools providing some sort of basic education. One is said to have been held in the cottage that later became White Hill Farmhouse. These were generally run by widows blessed with at least a rudimentary education, which they were prepared to pass on for a small fee.

Pitton and Farley would therefore seem to have been much better endowed with schools than were many villages. Perhaps we can give some credit to this enlightened attitude for the rather curious absence of villagers in the dock after the 1830 riots. On the other hand, it is noticeable that in the parish registers prior to about 1845 some of the men and most of the women getting married were unable to sign their name. 'Betty Pearce her mark X' was the formula.

In the 1851 census, just one year after the new school at Pitton was opened, two school-teachers are noted. One, evidently the head teacher, is Elizabeth Williams, aged forty-three, the childless wife of an agricultural labourer. The other is Emma Whitlock, a girl of sixteen. That seems to have been the standard arrangement for the rest of the century and indeed until at least the 1930s, when the author received his primary education there. The head teacher would have been qualified – at least, in the latter part of the period – but the junior would not. An exception occurred in the late 1870s and early 1880s, when Ted was a pupil there. The head was then a man, a Mr Taylor, whose whiskery figure appears in school photographs.

Of his schooldays Ted writes:

Education was a compulsory privilege that had to be paid for. The fee for labourers' children was one penny a week, for smallholder's children two pence, and for the children of better-off farmers and builders three pence. Our penny was paid by the parish. Every Monday morning after prayers all the children (except we little paupers) queued up before the teacher's desk to hand over the weekly fee. Woe to the child who had forgotten it! Back home to fetch it, straight away! No penny, no education!

The subjects taught at school were the three Rs – Readin', Ritin' and 'Rithmetic. We used to chant a little rhyme:

Our old maister's a jolly good man;
Tries to teach us all he can –

Readin', ritin', 'rithmetic –
An' he doan't fergit to use the stick.

There were less complimentary versions, of course.

The partition across the school served to separate the 'Little Room', where the infants were taught, from the 'Big Room'. When I was promoted to the Big Room I was given an exercise book – a brand-new one! This book, the only exercise book I ever had, was for copying select portions of my work on rare occasions, being for exhibition to the school inspector. Some promising pupils actually had two exercise books during their school career, but that was exceptional. For ordinary purposes we wrote on slates. In our pockets we carried a rag which, with the application of a little spittle, served to wipe the slate clean. It was also used as a handkerchief ...

The visitation by the Inspector provided an awful and majestic end to the school year, especially a pupil's last year. Our academic career came to an end when we reached 'the fourth standard', which we were expected to do when we were about twelve. The only reward for an industrious or intelligent child was that he was allowed to leave school a little earlier. Backward pupils were kicked out when they were about thirteen.

The test was not a written one but an oral examination conducted by the Inspector. Pressure on the pupils was as great as it is now when examinations loom. A child was never allowed to forget the great responsibility resting on him.

'Now, whatever thees do, thee be sure and mind to pass. I got a job looked out for thee, so don't thee *dare* come whoam and say thee's failed!'

The final weeks were filled by the time-honoured system of cramming. Knowledge was forced into unreceptive heads. Lessons were learned, parrot-like, and the cane was used liberally. The overriding necessity was that we should make a good impression when the great day came.

On the fateful morning we were dressed in our best clothes (if any), and our faces and boots were given an extra polish. At school, prayers were repeated and morning hymns sung in subdued and quavering voices, after which we awaited, in an agony of suspense, the arrival of the Inspector.

Presently a polished fly came clattering down White Way, to stop, with much jingling of harness, outside the school gate. An elderly gentleman in frock coat and top hat alighted. Only lords and rich men could afford a fly, while top hats and frock coats were as rare as Members of Parliament in Pitton.

We victims were impressed and not a little scared.

The mistress opened the door and curtsied deeply as the Great Man entered. We dithering pupils also bowed or curtsied, as we did when Lady Bathurst visited, only more reverently ... and our self-possession oozed away.

The rest of the day was a nightmare.

The Inspector glowered patronizingly and fired a question which had to be repeated several times before one girl hazarded a wrong answer. Whereat he frowned and made a note in a black book. All quaked. In the voice of the Big Bad Wolf coaxing Little Red Riding Hood, the Inspector exhorted us not to be afraid, and then shot out some more trick questions which we were too paralysed to answer. Joshua Fry, normally an intelligent boy, was asked to read aloud. He was given a travel book, which he held upside down. On this being pointed out to him, he hastily rectified his mistake and began to read: 'The skennery was rohmantic and pick-cherskew ...'

When it was time to write on our slates, we were so preoccupied in staring at the Inspector's magnetic figure and in considering the awful consequences of failure that we failed to pay much attention to the work in front of us.

Predictably, most of us failed, to the despair of the teacher and the apparent disgust of the Inspector (though perhaps his secret gratification, this being what he had expected all along).

However, there was scope for compromise. After all, these were only going to be farm workers and domestic servants. The annual quota of those permitted to leave school worked out about the same, year after year.

I managed to reach the goal of the fourth standard by the age of twelve and so left school at the end of the summer term. For a time it was a delight to me to walk past the school at play-time and poke my tongue out at old schoolfellows, still confined in the fenced enclosure, like chicken in a pen ...

It will not have escaped notice that, for one with such a rudimentary education, Ted has a fairly good command of the English language. With little else in the curriculum, other than one lesson in history and geography in alternate weeks, the pupils did receive a good solid grounding in 'Readin', Ritin', and 'Rithmetic'. On those foundations Ted built in the following years and for the rest of his life. He was a voracious reader. He also became a capable public speaker and local preacher, much appreciated for his sense of humour. He was always, though, poor at spelling – a fault not unheard-of in highly educated people today.

Before Ted went to day school, he attended Sunday School at the village chapel. On the whole, Pitton was a chapel village, perhaps very largely because it lacked a resident squire and parson. In their absence, every man was as good as his neighbour, and he took care that his neighbour knew it. It made for feuds and squabbles but also bred a race of opinionated, strong-minded characters, used to thinking for themselves. At various periods in history such villages were the nursery of Lollards, of Puritans, of Methodists, of trades unionists, of the Salvation Army and of sundry other progressive movements that at their birth caused consternation in the establishment. One of the achievements and crimes of the early Methodists was that they taught ordinary village lads to read, write and speak in public – a dangerous brew. George Loveless, leader of the Tolpuddle Martyrs, was a Methodist local preacher.

The women were also affected, not least of them the indomitable Jane, Daniel's wife.

Through the middle years of the nineteenth century Winterslow had an energetic and enlightened rector, the Revd Edward Luard. After helping village children with their education, he encouraged the girls to go into domestic service in London, arranging suitable posts for them and packing them off by the new train service. For years the villages around Salisbury were prolific recruiting-grounds for the swollen domestic staffs of Kensington, Chelsea and other fashionable suburbs. Included in the Winterslow recruits were Jane Noyce and her younger sister, Martha.

While they were living in London, the evangelist Charles Haddon Spurgeon (the Billy Graham of his day) was attracting huge congregations to his meetings at the Metropolitan Tabernacle, a building seating 6,000 and erected especially for him. His preaching had a strong appeal to young village girls such as these two, and it shaped them for life.

Back they came to Wiltshire, to conclude typical village marriages. The two sisters married two boys (Daniel and Arthur) who were cousins to each other and also cousins to the girls. Both set up house in Pitton and proceeded to try to mould their husbands into an acceptable pattern. Jane had more success than Martha. An exceptionally strong-minded person, she persuaded her wayward but malleable Daniel not only to become a chapel member but even to attempt preaching. Martha had less luck with Arthur, who was altogether a tougher character. Throughout his life he was a source of anxiety to his wife and daughters, three of whom became Salvation Army officers and were much concerned about the state of his soul. Perhaps they had reason. He was capable of greeting a respectable lady visitor with, 'Ah, old Bob got a bad bargain in thee. Thee bist a barrener. Back in my young days we made sure about a thing like that, avore we got married!'

'I han't bin all I might have bin,' he admitted once, not long before he died, 'but I han't bin all to the bad. Worryin' about my soul have kept they there womenfolk of mine out of mischief for the greater part of their lives!'

It might have been better for Daniel if he had been equally tough.

As it was, the formidable Jane had Ted to shape to her liking from the very beginning, and she made a thorough job of it. Ted recalls the Sunday routine:

> At eight o'clock the devout members met for a morning prayer-meeting, at which they prayed for God's blessing on the day's services. Mother used to go whenever possible and sometimes took us with her. Half-past nine saw us all at Sunday School. When, an hour later, morning service began, we simply changed our seats and stayed in the chapel till twelve o'clock. An hour's sermon was the rule rather than the exception …
>
> Most of the sermons weren't very interesting, being about such matters as justification by faith, sanctification and, of course, the ever-familiar hell fire, best described by a preacher who was also a blacksmith and based his graphic details on

his familiar forge fire. He it was who told us vivid stories of a wicked king, Nebuchadnezzar, who threw little boys into a fiery furnace, of poor little baby Moses found floating in a cradle among the rushes by a fair princess; of David who slew a giant with a catapult; and of the 'assassinationers' who brought in the head of John the Baptist on 'a gurt, big, yaller dish'.

I heard the story getting on for a dozen times, and the dish was always a 'gurt, big, yaller one'. Why, I could never discover.

Noisy preachers were to be preferred to quiet ones. The pulpit was a box-like contraption perched, without visible means of support, half-way up the front wall. When the old blacksmith came to preach, he caused the whole edifice to quiver and shake simply by stumping up the stairs, and when he really got going, the whole pulpit danced visibly beneath the pounding of his mighty fists. We waited on edge for the apparently inevitable collapse, but unfortunately it never happened.

The story of Jeremiah, as recounted by one emotional old woodman, lives in my memory.

'Well, my friends,' he began, 'we got old Jeremiah stuck fast in the mud, down in the miry pit. But never fear, my friends, we got an hour to get en out avore dinner-time.'

As he worked up towards the climax, the old fellow was quite carried away by excitement. His collar-stud broke loose from its moorings, allowing the collar to slip round to the back of his neck, where it stood upright. The sweat pouring down his face, he leaned over the edge of the pulpit, hauling hard at an imaginary rope.

'Here he comes, my friends! Here he comes! Heave hard! The ropes be holdin'. We'll have en out any minute now!'

There was this to be said for his style – the congregation never went to sleep during his sermons.

Singing at chapel was lusty. We went in for hymns with choruses. When I was a boy, many of the congregation couldn't read, and so the verses were beyond them, but they were able to join in the choruses. When the last verse was ended, they sang the chorus again, and again, and again, at full volume.

'I'm a pilgrim bound for glory,' they shouted, the tears streaming down their faces, while the red-faced cornet-blowers accepted to the best of their ability the challenge of the vocal uproar. We had a village band in those days, and most of the bandsmen were chapel people, so they took their instruments to the evening services. And old Harry Read used to bring along his violin too. A young lady was usually available to sit at the indifferent harmonium, though whether she hit the right notes was almost impossible to say.

Often in summer we had an open-air warm-up at the crossroads before the service, marching up the road to chapel in procession. It seemed to us the normal prelude to an evening service. That was why Charles Fry and his brother, who used to live at Pitton but had moved to Alderbury, took their cornets when in the 1880s they went to hear the Salvation Army hold one of its first services in Salisbury market-place. It seemed the natural thing to do. General William Booth knew a good thing when he heard about it, and so was born the first Salvation Army band.

Chapel people, of course, had no monopoly of music. Many village churches had an orchestra of flute, violin and cello, in fact, any musical instrument that happened to be available, including a 'serpent' (an ophecleide of sorts) and a barrel organ ...

Corroboration for Ted's memories comes from a hand-written document by an unknown writer, who states that he was born in 1861 and first went to the chapel Sunday School when he was nine years old. There were then some eighty or ninety scholars attending. He writes:

The old chapel was a very old-fashioned place. Free seats on one side for men, and free seats on the other side for women, who couldn't afford seat rent. The other seats were pews with doors. Each pew held five, and it had candles on each side of the entrance. There was no stove to warm the chapel, but the Methodists were very warm-hearted.

Every Good Friday we always had a tea meeting, and the Winterslow people always used to come down. Between tea and meeting time we had a good sing in the field close by. I've known the chapel full twice for tea. We had extra good missionary meetings and always good collections ... There were prayer meetings every Sunday morning at 8 o'clock and always a prayer meeting every Sunday night after the service ...

He concludes with the date of his conversion – 25 February 1876.

14 *Shepherd Boy*

When school-leaving time drew near, Ted's Uncle Arthur, who was then head shepherd to Farmer Parsons, had a word with widowed Jane.

'I be needin' a shepherd boy. Ted can come on wi' I. I'll mention it to the guvnor tomorrow.'

'Mention it' was the correct expression. Uncle Arthur, like all head shepherds, did much as he liked. No doubt in the course of conversation with his employer he brought in casually. 'Oh, young Ted, the widder's boy, will be startin' wi' I, the week atter next. I wants another boy, and he should do well enough.'

And that would be that. No farmer, in those days before the sheep industry had collapsed, would dream of questioning the decisions of a good shepherd, on whom the well-being of the flock and therefore of the farm depended. All he had to do was to pay the boy's wages.

Ted could not remember much about his first year as shepherd boy. He was, in fact, a general errand boy about the farm. He ran hither and thither all over the farm and village and, if others saved their legs at his expense, he at least had plenty of opportunities to savour life by making his journeys last longer than necessary. In the following year, though, he settled down in earnest to being apprentice shepherd.

Ted remembers:

For the first three months the daily work had little variety. On reaching the turnip field at seven o'clock in the morning Uncle Arthur and I first had to fill forty cribs with hay and carry them into the sheep pen. Then we pitched hurdles for a new fold and, finishing well before midday, admitted the sheep. Uncle Arthur made the holes for the posts, or 'shores', and I carried the 'shores' and hurdles to where they were needed. After a dinner of bread and cheese we spent an hour or two 'pecking' turnips out of ground with a 'turnip peck', so that the sheep could more easily nibble them. The day's work was completed by filling the cribs with hay again and carrying them to the folds for the sheep's supper. Not hard work, and very much to my liking. Better than school.

All went well until January, when one morning, after an overnight blizzard, we had to force our way to the folds through lanes buried in snowdrifts level with the tops of the hedges. The exposed fields had been swept bare by the wind, but most of the sheep were buried in snow that had drifted against the hurdles. We had a hard day's work, digging them out. Then the temperature fell, allowing the snow to hang around for more than a month. Many mornings I saw the sheep rise from the ground where they had been sleeping and leave pounds of wool frozen to the snow.

Still, having blistered my hands by seizing a frosted iron bar, I envied the sheep. They looked warmer than I was. My winter clothes were identical with my summer clothes, except that in addition I wore a scarf and an old overcoat. The overcoat was of unbleached calico soaked in boiling oil and lamp-black and was lined with horse-pad flannel. It smelt good but was poor protection against really cold weather.

Our first lambs were due on 8 February, so on the night of the 7th my uncle and I slept in the shepherd's hut, behind the straw-rick which formed one side of the lambing-pen. That is where we lived for the next five weeks. The hut was a kind of wooden box on iron wheels. Along one side of the interior was a ledge with clothes piled on it. This served as a bed for one of us. It would take two at a pinch, one with his head by the other's feet, but generally one of us lay on the clothes while the other dozed in front of the stove, where a fire burned day and night. The watchman went out to inspect the sheep at hourly intervals.

Even so, we sometimes found a new-born lamb nearly dead with cold and weakness. Then we brought the limp little body into the hut, wrapped it in sacking and laid it in front of the stove. That usually did the trick within about half an hour. If a lamb seemed to be dead, we buried it in a huge heap of hay at one end of the hut, pressing the hay down tightly all around it. It was surprising how often the apparent corpse revived.

We took special care of twins and triplets, for the reason that Uncle Arthur received a bonus of 1s.6d. for every lamb reared above the number of ewes kept. He used to aim for 500 lambs from his 400 ewes – technically a lambing average of 125 per cent.

One feature of this hard winter I found flattering. Waiting on Uncle Arthur and myself was priority work for three or four ordinary labourers. Every morning they brought us fresh supplies of hay, cake and water for the sheep, fuel for our stove and food and drink for ourselves. They were there to run errands, too, Uncle Arthur giving the orders. And if there were any rather unpleasant jobs to do, such as skinning a dead sheep, it was deputed to one of them.

'That's so that I don't carry any infection from it,' Uncle told me.

Later, though, I learned that it was a hangover from the bad old days, earlier in the century, when a shepherd with a hungry family might be strongly tempted to sacrifice a sheep now and again. So it became a strict rule that dead sheep were not the perquisites of the shepherd but had to be taken down to the farm.

I enjoyed that first lambing season, as I have every other lambing season since, even though I went without changing my clothes for weeks. To finish up with 900 sheep after starting with only 400 gave a real sense of achievement. One night I discovered where Uncle Arthur kept his whisky flask, tucked under the undercarriage of the hut, but an injudicious gulp put me off whisky for years!

Shearing

Victorian farmers reckoned that the wool clip should pay the wages of all the shepherds for a year. The shearing season was from the middle of May to early July. About three weeks before shearing, the sheep had to have their fleeces washed, for clean wool fetched 2 pence or 3 pence a pound more than unwashed.

Washing a flock of 400 or 500 sheep was a formidable

undertaking in Pitton's waterless valley, so the flock was taken to the nearest river, at Winterbourne.

Ted remembers:

> Between three and four o'clock on a May morning we started out from the farm. There were we three shepherds (for the farm had an assistant shepherd who looked after the other sheep when the ewes were lambing), three or four ordinary labourers, the sheep and a horse and cart loaded with provisions. We reached Winterbourne at about seven o'clock, when we all had breakfast, while the sheep had an hour's rest to cool down after their long walk.
>
> Farmer White over at Winterbourne kept a washing-pool in repair and charged visiting farmers a fee for the use of it. He had dammed a side-channel of the river to form a pool three or four feet deep, and had flung a hurdle across the channel a little way downstream to catch the sheep after washing.
>
> The sheep were admitted in small numbers to a pen on the edge of the pool. There they were seized by two stalwart labourers and hurled into the water. As they floated around, two other men scrubbed them with home-made tools consisting of cross-pieces of board nailed to the end of long poles, like hay-rakes without teeth. The washing over, the sheep floundered downstream until stopped by the hurdle. This enabled them to scramble to the bank, where they soon shook themselves dry ...

A somewhat similar performance, though without the presence of water, took place three weeks later, when the sheep were shorn. The venue was the central threshing-floor possessed by most farm barns of that time. In this operation the shearing was done by travelling gangs of specialists.

An examination of the censuses of the mid-century shows a big discrepancy between the number of Pitton men claiming to be agricultural labourers and the number employed on Pitton farms. In 1851, for instance, the census records 104 agricultural workers, but the village farms employ only forty-one. The other sixty-three were self-employed, casual workers. They were the natural heirs of the old independent peasantry dispossessed by the enclosures early in the century. Under the old order each would have had his little cottage holding, with an acre or so of land and well-defined rights on the commons. From this base he would be available to help with the seasonal work of the farms, such as hoeing, haymaking, harvest and threshing. It was the threatened loss of this last-named winter employment which sparked off the troubles of 1830.

As Victoria's long and peaceful reign brought increasing prosperity to England's farms, the erstwhile peasantry, now casual labourers, evolved a programme which offered them some sort of livelihood. Hoeing was undertaken by individual agreements between farmer and employees, sometimes by organized gangs. These latter did not confine themselves to local farms. They ranged far afield, sometimes penetrating as far as Surrey and Berkshire. In the 1890s Albert and John White, after spending the harvest period on Surrey farms, used to travel on to London, to see what offered in the metropolis. They said that, if the worst happened, they could always play their cornets, which they carried with them, in the streets. In other words, they went busking, and apparently did quite well at it.

Shearing was undertaken almost entirely by gangs, to one of which Ted and his Uncle Arthur attached themselves later in their career. In due course Uncle Arthur, predictably, became gang leader. Ted writes:

There were usually eight to twelve of us. We used to work from four o'clock in the morning to eight at night, with a half-hour's break for breakfast and tea and an hour for dinner (midday). We slept wherever we could, generally on a heap of straw in a barn, and by starting at four o'clock in the morning we were able to get in four hours work before breakfast. At least, that is what the older men, settling for a cold breakfast, did, but Uncle Arthur and my cousin Charlie and I preferred to get up at quarter-past-three and enjoy a cooked breakfast.

We lit a fire on the downland turf, at a safe distance from the barn, and hung our big iron kettle on a tripod over it. When the tongues of flame were merrily licking the kettle, we took rashers of bacon out of our rush baskets and, transfixing them on skewers cut from the nearest hedge, gathered round the fire to toast them.

I can see the scene now. Our gang of bearded men, their ragged coats tied by binder-twine around the waist, squatting close together on the dewy grass, the dancing flames throwing glows and shadows on our faces. As we slowly turn the skewers, the fat drops from the rashers, some into the fire and some onto slices of bread we hold out to catch it. The kettle begins to sing and rattle; the sheep are bleating impatiently in the barn; a lark wakes up and soars, singing, passing close overhead ...

Ted's eyes gleamed with nostalgia as he described the scene, and many a good tale could he tell of his life with the shearing gang. Naturally he became a very proficient shearer and more than once achieved the feat of shearing fifty sheep a day.

Towards the end of the century farm sales, fairs and markets which had been traditionally run by private treaty began to be taken over by auctioneers. By this time Arthur, Charles and Ted had graduated away from the shearing gangs and were specializing in preparing pedigree sheep, especially prize rams, for show and sale. They soon found themselves joining forces with one of the leading auctioneers, John T. Woolley of Salisbury, and became his right-hand men in arranging these events. And that is how Ted got his feet on the lower rungs of the ladder which led to his eventually becoming a farmer.

Threshing
By the 1880s the threshing-machines which had been the immediate cause of the riots of 1830 were an accepted part of farming equipment. They were still, however, somewhat rudimentary. They were not portable but were fixed to the central section – the old threshing-floor – of the great barn.

Power was supplied by a horse-gear. This was situated in a yard adjoining the barn. It consisted of a heavy disc, lying level with the ground and a few inches above it. Four wooden bars projected from the disc, at right angles to each other, and to these shafts the horses were harnessed. A spindle running along the ground connected the disc with the drum of the threshing-machine. The horses walking in a circle turned the disc and so provided the power for the machine.

Ted did not specialize as a shepherd straight away. There were times when he was called upon to do almost any farm job. For several months he led a team of horses for a ploughman, a job he disliked because of its monotonous repetition. And now and again he was given charge of the horses when threshing was in progress. About this job he writes:

> High above the disc was a small iron crow's-nest, called a 'cradle', in which stood the boy, myself, whose duty it was to keep the horses moving. Here, often in pouring rain or blizzards, I used to crouch all day, soaked to the skin and shivering, while the men threshed in the shelter of the barn. From time to time a sadistic character nicknamed Angel would poke out his head and shout, 'Now then, bwoy, touch they 'osses up a bit', just to keep me fully aware of my misery. My limbs became cramped and numb and afflicted with pins-and-needles. Beyond doubt, the days I spent driving the horse-gear were the most miserable of my whole life ...

It must have been not much later that this cumbersome contraption became obsolete. The future belonged, for a time, to the portable threshing-machine, hauled from field to field and from farm to farm, by an iron-wheeled steam-engine. This, in fact, was the standard machine for the job until after the Second World War.

Birds and Beasts
The improvement in firearms in the late eighteenth and early nineteenth centuries encompassed the doom of many familiar denizens of the countryside.

Roe deer were virtually extinct in the woods around Pitton and Farley at the beginning of the nineteenth century, the present flourishing population being descended from a reintroduction at Milton Abbas, Dorset, in the 1830s. Fallow deer continued to play an important part in the life of Cranborne Chase, on the borders of Wiltshire and Dorset, in the first half of the nineteenth century, to the extent that local poaching wars claimed frequent casualties, but most Wiltshire estates were given over to the cult of pheasants, and deer were regarded as a bit of a nuisance.

Foxes were now the quarry of those country gentry who enjoyed hunting and who must have had difficulties in reconciling the conflicting needs of foxes and pheasants. Most other wild animals were regarded as vermin. Churchwardens' account books for the eighteenth and the early part of the nineteenth centuries are awash with records of pence and shillings paid for sparrows, hedgehogs, badgers, 'moules' and 'poulcatts'.

The one exception was provided by hares, which were considered game, the taking of a hare being subject to the same penalties as taking a pheasant. Consequently they multiplied exceedingly, and William Cobbett, riding down the Avon valley in 1826, records with wonder that at Netheravon he saw 'an acre of hares'. He writes that the owner of the land ' ... took us into a wheat stubble close by his paddock; his son took a gallop round, cracking his whip at the same time; the hares (which were thickly in sight before) started up all over the field, ran into a flock like sheep; and we all agreed that the flock did cover *an acre of ground.*'

Classified natural history books of the nineteenth century tend to consist largely of lists of birds shot. Birds once common and familiar, such as kites, ravens, peregrine falcons, bustards and, indeed, most of the hawks and owls, were ruthlessly harried. The last pair of great bustards, once so well established on Salisbury Plain that the mayor of Salisbury used to include bustards in the menu for his inaugural feast, probably nested in Wiltshire before 1820. Writing in 1818, William Chafin gives an account of a bustard hunt on the downs near Winterslow Hut about fifty years earlier. He took a pot shot at one but failed to bag it. There were about twenty-five bustards in this flock, and Chafin rightly surmises, 'I believe such a number of bustards will never again be seen together in England.'

In the 'hungry forties' and earlier, small birds were for eating. As mentioned earlier 'Four-and-twenty blackbirds baked in a pie' were not pure imagination. Even sparrows were plucked and cooked, for the morsels of flesh on their breasts. Larks and wheatears, caught by shepherds in horsehair snares, were delicacies, to be sold rather than put into the cottage pot. There was also a demand for wild birds for cages. The last bird-catcher in Pitton was apparently Noah Whitlock, who operated until the first years of the present century. His victims were mainly goldfinches, bullfinches and linnets, – all good song-birds, A favourite method was to enclose a nest of fledglings in a cage, allowing the parent birds to feed them through the bars, but snares, decoys and bird-lime were also used.

During the middle years of the century, when English agriculture was striving its utmost to keep pace with the demands of the rapidly increasing urban population, much land was brought into cultivation probably for the first time since the Roman era. In particular, much downland was ploughed, and when farming fell into deep depression in the last decades, it was allowed to fall back into dereliction, often without even the benefit of being resown to grass. On such land, and because of the general neglect of the countryside, rabbits multiplied as never before. By close nibbling of any edible vegetation, they allowed the lowly plants of open ground to flourish, creating a habitat congenial not only to the rabbits themselves but also to downland birds, such as wheatears, which nested in old rabbit holes. Other birds now uncommon, such as stone curlew and red-backed shrikes, found the derelict countryside much to their liking.

With the present trend to intensive cultivation, these birds have become rare, but the disappearance of one species, the corncrake, remains a mystery. Until the end of the century it was an abundant summer visitor, to be found in every hayfield. Its raucous cries in spring were as familiar as those of the cuckoo, which arrived at about the same time. Now it has completely vanished from most of England. Attempts have been made to link its disappearance with the introduction of the mechanical grasscutter, replacing the traditional scythe, but no one is quite sure about it.

Sentimentality about birds is a recent development. Keats' romantic musings on the song of the nightingale were not shared by villagers in general. Their attitude was better expressed by a dialect poem, written in the 1920s, on the thoughts of a keeper living in a nightingale-infested wood.

A nightingale zat in an ole tharn bush
An zang nigh vit to bust en.
He oodn' gie I nar wink o' sleep
Till I got up and cussed en.

I tumbled out o' me jumbled bed
An' seized a china missile,
An', drowin' open the winder, said
I'll larn ee not to whissle.

An' I'd a-drowed en, that I sware,
If it hadn'a bin fer Mother;
She sez, Vayther, doan' ee chuck that there,
Cos we han't got nar nuther!

Changing Pasture.

15 These Were Victorian Villagers

The England of the first decades of the nineteenth century
is hardly recognizable as the England of the last decade, so
vast is the chasm between them. As the sun rose on the
first days of the new century, it shone on a country in
which the gap between an affluent and apparently
unassailable ruling class and an anonymous proletariat
was as deep as ever it had been.

At the lowest levels it was a drunken, barbaric England
in which the threat of the hangman's rope dangled as the
penalty for scores of minor offences. Bull-baiting and
cock-fighting awoke no qualms of conscience. Man-traps
and spring-guns made a walk in woods hazardous.
Orphans were sent to clamber up hot chimneys; small
children worked for unreasonable hours in factories and
mines; work in the slave plantations of the West Indies
was a fate to which many an Englishman was condemned.
It was an England familiar enough to readers of Dickens,
but Dickens still lay half a century ahead. Things were far
worse in the early 1800s. Moreover, it was an England at
war.

By the end of the century immense changes had
occurred. The Reform Acts had done their work,
abolishing the ancient monopoly of the country
gentleman in public affairs, yet without violent revolution.

The revolution had, indeed, been industrial, ushering in a new era of unprecedented prosperity based on manufacturing-industries. Wars were still fought only on foreign soil; in England a profound peace reigned.

A dominant feature of this new order was the emergence of a rapidly growing middle class. Like England's new civilization, it was preponderantly urban, but it affected every village in the land. The old apartheid system gradually faded away. Above all, new humane attitudes prevailed. It was an age of philanthropy, characterized by concern for the poor and unfortunate and, in another sphere, by the 'restoration' of innumerable derelict churches.

It is true that in the last two decades of the Victorian era agriculture was in the doldrums again. Landowners, farmers and labourers found themselves the victims of forces they could not understand. Even that, however, brought them closer together. They all suffered, but not so comprehensively as in past depressions, for they were just unfortunate units in an economy which was booming.

Village life was much as it was in the first half of the twentieth century, before it was taken over by suburbia. Most of us either lived in that environment or had parents, grandparents or other relations who did. We can, to some extent, identify ourselves with our ancestors of the 1890s. And many of us attempt to do so. There is a flourishing cult of family history research, of the search for ancestors. From 1850 onwards it is not very difficult, and the people we discover are not very different from ourselves. Before 1850 the way is beset with doubts and uncertainties, and the individuals whose names we find in yellowing registers are not ones with whom we can readily identify.

So when we take note of Victorian villagers, we tend to look at those nearest to us in time and outlook. There is an abundant choice. Here we salute just a few examples of them from our Victorian village, taken not so much at random as because they may have something to say to us. Their common denominator is that they were 'characters'.

But first, one from the 'dark ages', from the early part of the century.

The Witch

Although Lyddie Shears was a Winterslow woman, she was widely known in the district, and, in fact, her story has become a part of Wiltshire folklore.

Apparently she was a market woman, who used to obtain stock at Romsey market and then hawk it around Winterslow. Fostering a reputation for possessing the evil eye, she found a ready sale for her goods, many cottagers being scared to refuse her.

The Winterslow Women's Institute scrapbook quotes poachers as saying that,

> If they took Lyddie baccy and snuff she would go out with flint and steel, striking sparks which attracted hares so that the poachers could knock them over. The legend is that she so teased a Farmer Tanner by turning herself into a hare for him to course with his greyhounds, the hare always disappearing in her garden, that the farmer sought the advice of the Rector of Tytherley. The good man recommended that a bullet be made of a sixpenny-piece. The farmer with it shot the elusive hare, and the witch was found dead in her cottage with a silver bullet in her heart!

Edith Olivier, the Wiltshire historian, elaborates: 'The hare was shot dead as it entered her garden. But afterwards, as they called at the cottage, they saw the body of Lyddie Shears lying on the floor dead, and upon examination the silver bullet was found to have caused her death.'

The truth of the matter is impossible to determine. One wonders, for instance, who on earth carried out the post mortem to discover the fatal bullet. In fact, similar stories, including the detail of the silver bullet in the heart, are told about alleged witches in other parts of England. Lyddie Shears and her reputation for witchcraft are, however, undoubted facts.

Nor is the belief in the power of witches entirely dead. Within the author's fairly recent memory, a married couple kept secret from an older member of the family, who they feared was a witch and whom they thought they might have offended, the news that the wife was pregnant. Having already a family of two girls, they badly wanted the new baby to be a boy, and they were scared that the suspect witch would cast a spell and cause it to be another girl!

Hares were, of course, sacred and magical animals in Celtic mythology, and superstitions about them lingered until very recent times – perhaps still do.

A curious story relates to Arthur Whitlock, a celebrated (or notorious) poacher of hares throughout most of his life. During his last illness he was lying in bed in his home, Willow Cottage, Pitton. He was alone in the house, but, it being a warm summer afternoon, the doors and windows had been left open. A hare came in through an open door, ran upstairs to the main bedroom and stood for a minute, looking at the old man in bed. Then it jumped out of the window.

When his daughter Susie returned he told her of the incident, concluding, 'Well, that's it! I shall soon be going home now!' And within a week he was dead.

For a hare, one of the most timid of wild creatures, to venture into a house, is almost unheard-of. But did it really happen? Or did the old man dream it? Or invent the story, pulling his daughter's leg, as he so often did?

'He seemed convinced that the hare had been sent to summon him,' she used to say. 'But *I* don't know!'

Emmanuel Parsons

In the transition from the bad old days of the early 1800s to the evening calm of the 1890s, a leading role was undoubtedly played by Emmanuel Parsons. More than anyone else he was responsible for the development of harmonious relations between the, at times, bitterly antagonistic elements that comprised the population of Pitton and Farley. For instance, he had much to do with the establishing of friendly relations with two of the parish's most relentless critics whom we have already met, Samuel Lampard, the Baptist preacher, and James Parsons, the 'extreme radical agnostic'. By inviting them to join a newly created school board, he converted these two to becoming willing and staunch supporters of himself and the vicar in sundry improvements that were being effected.

Emmanuel, born in 1846, was the only son of a farmer, tenant of 130 acres, at The Livery, Winterslow. He was descended from an ancient farming family in Farley. The unusual Christian name, Emmanuel, was traditional in the family, though an entry in a document dated soon after the Enclosures of 1810 reveals a curious anomaly. One of four parishioners granted exemption from the roads rate, amounting to about 2 shillings, on the grounds of poverty, was Emmanuel Parsons. However, there were several families of Parsons in Pitton and Farley in those days, and this looks like one of the poorer relations deliberately cashing in on the name, in the hope that some benefit might one day accrue to the lad!

At any rate, our Emmanuel took over the farm on his father's death in 1865, when he was only nineteen. In 1869 he was appointed steward of the Earl of Ilchester's Pitton and Farley estates, a post he held until the estates were sold in 1912. Throughout those years he farmed extensively on his own account and for much of the time served the community in almost every available capacity. He was churchwarden, member of the parish vestry, official collector of rates, taxes and tithes, member of the board of guardians and later of the local councils which succeeded them. He was slim, handsome, energetic (a great walker), diplomatic, fair in his dealings with rich and poor and deeply involved in most local affairs, including the church choir, for he had a good singing voice.

Villagers now dead but once known to the author remembered him with respect and sometimes affection. To them he was never 'Mr Parsons' but always 'Farmer Emmanuel' or, more often, 'Farmanuel'. Not the least of his achievements was to keep a meticulously detailed diary for all those years – a treasure-house for historians.

The Revd John Messenger

John Messenger was curate of Pitton and Farley in 1864 and became first vicar of the new parish of Pitton and Farley in 1874. Through those middle years of the century he worked closely with Farmer Emmanuel, and evidently they made a strong team. He lived with his wife at the Wardenry, where they raised seven children, and was, by all accounts, a very friendly and generous man. The whole family was musical. They founded an excellent choir, bought the church a new harmonium to replace the old barrel-organ and arranged a programme of concerts every winter.

It so happened, however, that John Messenger had been brought up in luxury. He was the only son of a prominent civil servant who had retired on the then enormous pension of £1,200 a year, from which he evidently contributed generously to the support of the Farley family. Unfortunately for them, when the old man died, so did the pension. From being able to keep 'a carriage and coachman, gardener, cook, parlour-maids and nurses', they sank into poverty. They had no idea how to adapt to the changed circumstances. All the staff were dismissed one by one, the horses and vehicles were sold and still the family sank into debt.

Eventually the Messengers were virtually bankrupt. A meeting of creditors in Salisbury agreed to accept 10 shillings in the pound if they could be assured of that amount within a reasonable time. John Messenger decided to move away and secured the living of a parish near Manchester. It is good to know that, despite all his financial troubles, the parishioners of the two villages subscribed to present him with a clock on his leaving the parish. The presentation, with appropriate expressions of thanks, was made by his old opponent, Samuel Lampard. And when, nearly thirty years later, he died at his Lancashire parish, Farley sent a message to his family, assuring them that the parishioners remembered him 'with the greatest affection and respect'.

The episode had, of course, a temporarily adverse effect on the church. 'Several people felt they should no longer go to church when their bills were not met,' noted Emmanuel Parsons, 'and they became active supporters of Methodism. Some others refused to go to church; others compromised and ended up by going nowhere.'

The shortcomings of religious adherents are always an unsound excuse for changing one's allegiance, as is illustrated by our next characters.

The Pitts and the Brieants

In the mid-Victorian years two firms of builders and wheelwrights established themselves at Pitton. According to the 1851 census, Jeremiah Brieant was then a master builder employing ten men. Stephen Pitt is classified as a master carpenter without employees, though with two sons, John and George, working with him. The Pitts, prospering, eventually moved to Fordingbridge and then to Amesbury, where their descendants still run a flourishing garage. It was the Brieants who opened and for a time operated the lime-kilns by White Hill, though it seems that they were reviving an industry that had functioned there at an earlier date.

Both Brieants and Pitts were members of the chapel at Pitton (the pre-1888 building). In those days the box pews near the pulpit could be rented, while those who could not afford such luxuries sat on bare benches at the back. Reminiscences recall rivalry between the female members of the Brieants and Pitts, vastly to the entertainment of the paupers at the back, who poked fun at the extravagant hats flaunted by the ladies as they sailed up the aisle.

Unfortunately for them, or at least for the Brieants, a disaster similar to that of the Messengers befell them. Under the control of Jeremiah's son, Lewis, the business over-extended itself. Emmanuel Parsons records that on 19 January 1887 Lewis '... left his home this morning, telling his wife he should be back about three o'clock, but he did not return at all. I understand his horse was left at Mr Hemmings stables, but I do not know what became of his trap. His brother came over on Thursday and discharged his carpenter and blacksmiths and closed the shops. I hear his wife is in a great way about it and did not go to bed till 12 o'clock the next day. Money difficulty is the cause of his going, I believe.'

He was right. The family faced financial ruin. Lewis, in fact, refused to face it. He had gone to Southampton and taken ship for New York. Hearsay has it that he never came back but later established contact with his family from America.

It is to be hoped that, church and chapel having each faced a similar crisis within a few years, the members benefited from the experience and faced up to the future with increased charity and humility. Indeed, the record of improving tolerance seems to indicate that they did.

Since writing the above the author has received, from America, further information of the Brieant family saga.

Evidently in the 1880s the Brieant business at Pitton was run by two of Jeremiah's grandsons, Charles and Lewis. Charles seems to have concentrated on the farming side of it, Lewis on the building, including the lime-kilns.

The story is that in due course the lease of the lime-kilns, which were on the Earl of Ilchester's property, expired. The Earl offered a new lease at a greatly increased rent, which Lewis indignantly refused and gave notice to quit. After some acrimony the Earl offered Lewis a renewal of the lease on the original terms, but Lewis stubbornly refused to accept them. By 1887 the building business was in a bad way, and Lewis absconded to America. The linked farming enterprise also foundered and Charles finished his career managing other people's farms.

In America Lewis made his base with relations already in residence there. He was soon involved in building and was engaged in the construction of some of the major structures in New York's Central Park. In due course his wife and children emigrated to join him, as did some of his Brieant nephews. His descendants are still there, many of them in New York State and New Hampshire. They include several doctors and bankers, and a distinct line of musical ability runs through the family.

Our picture of Jeremiah Brieant is from an oil painting in the possession of an English member of the family, now living in Lincolnshire, who also treasures some letters about him. He was, she says, a very cheerful soul, as his portrait indicates. She adds:

> One incident relates how he was caught in a heavy thunderstorm in Salisbury. He went into Style & Gerrish's and bought a blanket, wrapped in which he drove home. He said he had plenty of jackets at home, but a blanket would always come in useful!
>
> On completing the building of his house, now 'The Silver

Plough' at Pitton, he is said to have drunk beer from a chamber-pot sitting on the top of one of the chimneys!

Helen Fry

Contemporary records of life in a Victorian village were, understandably, written mainly by people in the upper echelons of village society. First-hand documents throwing light on the realities of life for the very poor (who, after all, constituted the great majority of villagers) are rare – which, of course, enhances the value of Ted Whitlock's memoirs. Some reminiscences of a sort, penned by Mrs Helen Fry in her old age, therefore have considerable interest. They are concerned primarily with her spiritual life but include some revealing practical information. Helen was a member of an old Pitton family and was a contemporary of old Donkey Bill and his son Daniel. She writes:

> My husband, being a gamekeeper, had gone out shooting with some gentlemen, and I never saw him again alive. The morning he went out it began to snow, and as the day advanced it fell thicker and faster. As the evening drew on I began to get anxious for his return. All night long I watched and waited, but, alas! he came not, till in the morning he was borne in on a stretcher. He had perished in the snow ...
>
> This was indeed a sad trial for me. Left with ten fatherless children, the youngest but four months old, I found Mrs Young a great comfort to me. I met with much sympathy in the village. The ladies especially flocked around me to render such assistance as lay in their power. I gained a living by needlework; the ladies were very kind and kept me well supplied with work ...

No compensation was either expected or received from the keeper's employers. No one saw anything wrong or unusual in a widow with ten small children having to set to and earn a living for them. The thing to do was to help her by providing plenty of work. Helen was lucky in choosing sewing rather than laundry. A more usual procedure would have been for the villagers to subscribe for a mangle.

Incidentally, Fry's death must have occurred in January 1881, the blizzard being one of the most severe for the whole century. A contemporary diary records: 'About 7.a.m. on the 18th it began to snow, which continued the whole day, drifting frightfully. It was so cold and the wind so rough, one could not look up against it. There was a cessation about midnight for two or three hours, after which it came on thicker than before, and did not cease for the whole of the 19th ... No man living could remember two days of such weather in succession. Roads blocked, and all business at a standstill ... It is estimated that 100 people perished in the storm.'

Working with her needle, Helen Fry managed to support her family for nine years. Then she married again – to a widower with two small children of his own!

Writing in her old age, just before the First World War, she commented: 'It is rather lonely here, and I am shut in from the outside world, but I do not mind. I am very thankful to have the old-age pension – four shillings a week is a great help – for which I thank God, knowing He is the giver of all good ...'

Lloyd George, who had just introduced old-age pensions for the first time, might have felt a little aggrieved at not sharing the credit.

On the same page, with a touch of her old spirit, she notes, 'A Salvation Army officer also called, this being self-denial week. I told him I had had to practice self-denial every day of my life!'

What she does not record is her work with other village wives. When she had settled down to her sewing routine, she began to invite her neighbours to join her in afternoon meetings in her cottage. They were primarily religious meetings, with Bible readings and prayer, but hordes of small children came along with their parents and were regaled with stories. No doubt there was much local gossip as well. Helen's cottage became the centre of much of the social life of the village – at the farm-labourer level.

When she died, in 1916, Pitton Methodists erected a tablet in the chapel to her memory. It reads

IN MEMORY OF
HELEN FRY,
for Years
CLASS LEADER AND SCRIPTURE READER

who entered into rest
July 12th, 1916
'She being dead, yet speaketh'.

Mary Batten

Mary Batten, who lived at Farley at the end of the nineteenth century, was evidently a woman of similar character. A diarist, quoted by Michael Parsons, calls her 'dear old Mary Batten' and writes of her:

> She invariably wore an old-fashioned sun bonnet and a large shawl. Surely never has a parish had a woman with a heart so full of kindness and genuine goodness. Very poor (as we all were) but spotlessly clean, she was ever ready and pleased to go to the help of anyone in need of help. In any case of sickness or accident or where a little extra help was required with household chores and most frequently when there was a confinement it was 'Send for Old Mary'. She was soon at hand, and only in very exceptional circumstances would she expect or even accept any payment.
>
> 'No, no, I don't want no pay. Surely neighbours can do a good turn without being paid for it,' she would say. Most of the old cottagers were moved by the same spirit – whatever your trouble might be, you always knew that a good neighbour would be at hand, ready and willing to help out.

James Barnett

He is classified as a shoemaker, and he did indeed make shoes as well as mend them. Girls used to complain that his shoes, of heavy utility types made for hard wear, never wore out!

He lived at Pitton in one of the two thatched cottages later amalgamated to form Taylor's Farmhouse, and an apple tree he planted in the garden still flourishes. On Sundays he conducted services in Methodist chapels in the Salisbury Circuit and had a reputation as a notable preacher. His working day began at four o'clock in the morning, and, by rota, each of his four daughters had to rise with him and read the Bible to him for four hours till breakfast-time at eight o'clock! Those who knew him said that he was a dear old man but that his wife was a bit of a dragon.

A surviving Salisbury Circuit plan records James

Barnett's preaching appointments for the quarter from November 1874 to 7 February 1875. They were at chapels at Winterslow, Idmiston, West Dean, Pitton (his home church), Broughton, Winterbourne, Farley and West Grimstead. In each case he was expected to conduct two services, one in the morning and one in the evening, someone in the village congregation supplying hospitality. Most appointments involved a journey of from two to four miles each way, James walking to them, of course, in his home-made boots. The journey home in this quarter was inevitably in darkness. He was, of course, only one of thousands of local preachers with such a Sunday schedule before the age of motor-cars.

Abraham Collins

A member of the numerous Collins clan, Abraham comes into our story for one reason only. He took part in a cricket match between Pitton and Farley on 6 October 1866.

This was an all-day match, played in a field called Howe for a barrel of beer. Who won was not recorded, but in the 1920s or 1930s, Pitton Cricket Club being short of funds decided that a centenary match would be a good idea. No one knew just when the centenary was, so a date was fixed arbitrarily and an enjoyable match was played. Indeed, so popular was it that it was repeated on several subsequent occasions, regardless of the fact that centenaries come round only once in a hundred years!

Then someone remembered the story that Abraham Collins, playing for Pitton, was called away before the match ended and certainly before the barrel of beer was broached, to go home to his wife who had just given birth to her first baby. That baby was Reuben Collins. So all that was necessary was to check on Reuben's age and birthday, and the date of the cricket match was revealed. It was 6 October 1866. The Cricket Club was none too pleased with the informant. He had killed their excuse for lucrative centenary matches.

Incidentally, the date, 6 October, is worthy of note. Cricket fixture lists have usually ended by the end of September, but the organizers evidently knew that it was useless to arrange an all-day match while there was a chance of harvest not being finished.

Both Pitton and Farley were cricketing villages. There is an early record of a cricket club's existing at Pitton, and on Saturday 24 May 1834 a match was played on West Dean race-course between Farley and East Grimstead. It was evidently an all-day match, for two innings were completed by both sides. East Grimstead won.

Moses Welstead

Moses Welstead of Farley had a reputation of being 'a very clever man with all sorts of beasts, as good as any vet'. Emmanuel Parsons' diaries pay frequent tribute to his skill. He was also a character very similar to 'dear old Mary Batten', for Emmanuel records that, 'He always utterly refused to accept any payment for services, saying, "Twould be hard lines if we couldn't help a poor animal without being paid for it." '

William Baugh

William Baugh was the son of a Winterslow farm-worker who had come to live in Pitton and whose home was in a thatched cottage where Cherry Tree Cottage now stands. In his old age William remembered an occasion when three of his small sisters were lying dead in the cottage at once, the victims of an epidemic of fever.

As a young man he went out of curiosity to the first Salvation Army meetings in Salisbury and was attracted by what he saw. Joining the Army, he was soon engaged in its campaign in the East End of London, protecting the Salvationist lassies from the attacks of thugs by laying about him with his big carriage umbrella. He was a strong, muscular Christian. Later he rose to the rank of brigadier and was entrusted with the task of establishing the Army's work in America. He used to relate how once, in the backwoods of Maine, he met a woman who, like himself, had been converted in Pitton Chapel.

Other Old-timers

George White

One feels one would like to know more about old George

White of Farley. In 1879 he was threshing seven sacks of oats with a flail, for Farmer Emmanuel. And when the new harmonium was installed in the church, he is noted as the old chap who used to play the barrel-organ. At the time of his death, in December 1885, he was the parish sexton.

Chunky Garrett

Chunky Garrett is remembered for the circumstances of his death, on 27 December 1883. He had been '... keeping up Christmas by singing at different houses in the parish and had too much to drink, so that he was very drunk, and in that state lay down in the field (Little Common, near Crossways, Farley) and never woke again, due to exposure to the cold ...'.

Billy Lazarus

His real name was Fry. He lived at Pitton but disappeared one day, and the rumour spread that he had died. Some years later he suddenly returned, but he would never give any information about where he had been. So the villagers, likening him to Lazarus who rose from the dead, thereafter always referred to him as 'Billy Lazarus'.

Jesse Whitlock

A younger brother of Arthur Whitlock, he met with an accidental death in about 1870, when aged twenty-one. Working with a horse and cart in the field known as Jenningses, about a mile out of the village along the Winterslow Hill road, he pulled a loaded gun muzzle-first out of the cart. The charge of shot blew a hole in his upper arm, just below the armpit. He ran the mile from the field to Pitton, where the carrier harnessed horse and van to take him to Salisbury Infirmary. No one in the village had the skill to apply a tourniquet or to take any other effective measures to staunch the flow of blood, so he bled to death before he arrived at the hospital.

John Webb

Like Helen Fry, John Webb is honoured by a marble tablet in Pitton chapel. Through the last decade of the nineteenth century and the first two decades of the twentieth he was Sunday School superintendent and class leader and was held in high esteem in the village. He

was an agricultural labourer and, in his later years, the
village roadman.

It is interesting to note that in the new chapel (erected in
1888) rows of initials displayed prominently over the
pulpit commemorate those who made handsome contri-
butions to the new building – who, in fact, 'purchased a
stone'. The initials of Helen Fry and John Webb are not
there. At that time more than half the population bore the
surnames White, Whitlock, Williams and Webb, most of
them known Methodists, yet only one 'W' appears in the
list. The explanation is that most of these were
farm-workers, who, with the best will in the world, could
not afford to lay a foundation stone.

Albert Shears
A frequent visitor to Pitton and Farley in the last decade of
the nineteenth century was Albert Shears of Winterslow,
in his Gospel Mission Caravan. A man of strong
evangelical views, he found himself in disagreement with
the members and doctrines of all the churches and chapels
in the villages and so founded his own mission, which still
survives in the flourishing Gospel Lifeboat Mission in
Winterslow. His well-equipped and brightly painted
caravan was a familiar sight in the neighbouring villages.

Planting
Potatoes

16   The Daily Round

We have some notes of a conversation, in the 1920s or 1930s, with an old lady reminiscing about her daily life in the 1880s. She was the wife of a small farmer – someone like Elisha Whitlock.

> The week was mapped out for us in advance. When a girl married she knew just what awaited her on each day of the week for the rest of her life.
>
> Monday was wash-day. Tuesday was ironing day. Wednesday was bedroom day. Thursday was cooking day. Friday was cleaning and polishing day. Saturday was preparation for the Sabbath. Cooking day and cleaning day could be interchangeable, but a routine, once established, was immutable. Only a crisis, such as the arrival of a baby, allowed any alterations, and even then whoever looked after you when you were in bed followed the same routine.
>
> What a battle wash-day used to be! Up before daybreak and getting the fire under the copper lighted. I could start it up with some kindling wood and some embers from the hearth fire. But if the hearth fire had gone out overnight, then I had to get out the old tinder-box, and that was a job, I can tell you! Sometimes it would take me twenty minutes or more to strike a light ...

Twenty minutes to achieve a result which takes us only seconds, by striking a match or flicking an electric switch!

Our copper really was made of copper. It was set back in a recess of the wall of the old kitchen that doubled up as a dairy. I put the clothes in the copper, and while it was heating up I got busy preparing the starch. Two tablespoons of starch into the bowl, and stir up. And the blue-bag handy to dab on wasp stings and insect bites.

When the clothes were ready I fetched them out with the copper stick and dumped them in the tub for rinsing. Two lots of rinsing, in blue water; then through the mangle and out on the clothes'-line to dry.

Old Maud, who lived next door, used to go along the road to help her niece, Susie, who had eleven children, on Monday mornings. That was Susie Metcalf. Her man was a farm worker, and they had only a two-bedroomed cottage, with one living-room downstairs and a tiny kitchen, so there wasn't room indoors for the copper. They had an old fireplace rigged up under a lean-to outside the back door, and that's where Susie and Auntie Maud did their washing – for eleven children.

Mind you, when we'd done our main wash and got the clothes on the line, we hadn't finished. There were all the outdoor clothes to wash, and all the farm sacks. We used the same water for that. Never do to waste water, 'cos it all had to be drawn up from the well, by windlass. By the time I'd finished washing a dozen or two tatie sacks the water was half-mud. But it was all the better for watering the garden.

Of course, the water for Monday wash-day had to be drawn on Saturdays. Mustn't do it on Sundays. That was the man's job, Saturday afternoons.

I remember the old wash-day rhyme we used to recite:

They that wash on Monday have all the week to dry.
They that wash on Tuesday do not go far awry.
They that wash on Wednesday are not so much to blame.
They that wash on Thursday, wash for shame.
They that wash on Friday, wash in need.
And they that wash on Saturday are dirty sluts indeed!

... I got reason to remember one wash-day. 'Twas one of those blowy Monday mornings, when the wind had got round west after overnight rain. Good drying weather. I'd just got all the clothes nicely pegged on the line, reaching from the back door right down to the orchard, and they were all billowing out lovely in the wind – it was a big wash day that day, I remember, when the clothes-post snapped off! There, I knew it was getting the worse for wear, and I'd told my man about it. Been on at him for weeks about it, I had, and every time he'd say, 'Yes, I'll see to it. Don't you worry.'

I suppose it was the weight of the clothes and the buffeting the wind was giving them. Anyway, off it snapped, and there went the clothes, all over the garden. Over the sprouts and the taties and the dahlyers and the wet grass – all my morning's work! – all my lovely clean sheets! – trailing in the mud!

Then round the corner of the house came these two blessed dogs, gambolling with their dirty feet all over my clean sheets, all over my clean sheets. And after them, his lordship! 'Hey, Mother,' he says, 'can I have an early dinner today … hullo, what's up here?'

That's when I hit him. It's the only time in my married life I ever hit him, and I was sorry for it afterwards. But I couldn't help it. I just couldn't help it! …

Hop-Picking.

17   Uncle Jim

Daniel Whitlock had two sisters, Phillida and Susannah. Of Susannah, the younger, Ted Whitlock knew little, except the laconic information that, 'She married Harry Saunders, a carpenter, and died with a county court summons in her pocket.'

Phillida occupied a more prominent place in his life. Her husband was James Parsons, a man of remarkable vision and some ability. James, whose relationship to other members of the large Parsons family is uncertain, lived at Farley and was much involved in public affairs. He was village correspondent for Pitton and Farley for the local papers, balancing his reporting of village events with thought-provoking articles mainly on political subjects. He was very friendly with Edward Slow, the Wilton dialect poet, a man of almost – though not quite – the calibre of William Barnes, whose work survives in several volumes of verse preserved in Wiltshire libraries. Slow dedicated a poem to James.

Evidently James and Samuel Lampard, the tenants of Farley Farm, represented the radical element in the parish in the 1860s and 1870s, often finding themselves in bitter opposition to the establishment. Samuel Lampard is on record as being a Baptist local preacher, and presumably he was the Farmer Lampard of whom William Whitlock, the Winterslow farmer, fell foul in the poaching incident of 1852, related in Chapter 11. James, on the other hand, is said to have been 'an extreme radical agnostic', though there seems to be some doubt about this. A writer of a history of a suburb of Calgary, Canada, where James settled in 1886, says that, 'Mr Parsons was a local preacher and took quite an interest in church and Sunday School work.' Perhaps both versions are correct; perhaps he and Emmanuel Parsons changed their ideas after settling in a new land.

Back in Farley in the 1870s a new vicar, the Revd J.F. Messenger, converted the two dissidents, Samuel Lampard and James Parsons, from being vigorous opponents to enthusiastic supporters by offering them positions of managers on a newly formed board to control Farley Church of England School. This enlightened vicar also founded a reading-room, of which James thoroughly approved and made full use.

James was born at either Pitton or Farley in 1850 and apparently started his working life as a farm-labourer at the age of twelve or thirteen. Like his nephew Ted some twenty years later, he then continued his education by voracious reading and acute observation. He was what the villagers called a 'bookish lad'. He much preferred to sit and read rather than get on with the work of the farm. Consequently he soon acquired a reputation for laziness.

He wandered about from job to job, accustomed to abuse and not greatly worrying about it. He could withdraw at will into a private world of his own. He taught himself shorthand and began to send letters and reports to the local papers. The editor of the *Salisbury Times*, a Mr William Wells, recognized his talent and encouraged him. Frequent articles by James Parsons began to appear in the paper. In 1869 he was stirred by the case of two children who were imprisoned in Fisherton Anger gaol for 'stealing turnip-greens' from a field on Bishopdown Farm, just outside Salisbury. Mr Wells and James, together with a Member of Parliament, a Mr Peter Taylor, conducted a campaign which led to their release. Soon afterwards Mr Wells offered James a job as a reporter, on the understanding that it was simply a step on the way to something higher.

But James had other ideas. He joined the Workmen's Peace Association of England, which advocated the reduction of armaments and the formation of an international organization such as the League of Nations eventually became. From his immense range of borrowed literature he had been fired by a vision of the expanding British Empire, then nearing its zenith. In the peaceful world of the future, the British Empire, standard-bearer of the new morality, had necessarily to play a leading part.

Throughout the middle years of the nineteenth century the impetus given to emigration by the forced exile of the 1830 rioters continued to grow. Most of the emigrants were still country folk, in search of land on which to settle and raise families. Australia was a first choice, but in the late 1870s and early 1880s the steady penetration westwards of the Canadian Pacific Railway across the prairies opened up a vast new territory. Huge numbers of settlers poured westwards, among them James and Phillida Parsons.

James wrote: 'These great new countries of Canada, Australia, New Zealand, South Africa and the rest will inevitably support a huge population in years to come. They will become great nations. At present they are British, but if they are to remain so they must receive liberal transfusions of British blood. Otherwise other nationalities will populate the empty spaces, and the Empire will disintegrate.'

He had other visions of the future too. In the early 1880s he was writing of the part to be played by air power in a future war. He foresaw men tapping new sources of power in the strata beneath the chalk, with the result that southern England, including Pitton and Farley, would become industrial. He prophesied that the capital of the Empire would eventually be moved to Canada – a prophecy which was nearly fulfilled in 1940.

James's motives were altruistic. He writes, 'I was married on December 6th, 1882, at the Registry Office at Richmond, near London, to Phillada [as he spells the name] Whitlock, who fully expected that her future life would be short and her married part of that not likely to exceed a few years.' (It lasted, in fact, for more than forty years.) The reason for such pessimism is unknown but it may have been connected with her inability to bear children. She and James neither expected nor achieved a family. Their Canadian-born son, Edward, was adopted.

In April 1886 James and Phillida took train to Liverpool and there embarked on a ship for Canada, their many friends in Pitton, Farley and Winterslow wishing them Godspeed. Travelling westwards on the Canadian Pacific Railway, they alighted at Calgary. The mushrooming township was on land largely granted to the railway, whose directors sold it off in parcels to individuals. A search of the early records has failed to discover any such grant to James Parsons, but he could well have bought his farm from someone who could not keep up his payments – apparently a frequent occurrence.

It has been possible to locate his holding – a quarter-section – on an old map. It seems, in fact, to consist of parts of two quarter-sections, one of which he shares with a Mr E. Budd, the other with Harry Collicutt. It lies in the southern part of Calgary, and one of the main runways of Calgary Airport runs diagonally right across it. A stream, the Nose Creek, wriggled from north to south along the edge of the land, and an intrusive swamp caused James and his fellow settlers much trouble in the early days. In about 1900 they undertook a quite formidable drainage scheme which was not entirely successful until some years later.

In his letters to relations back in Britain, James was fond of reminding them that, although his farm was on comparatively level terrain, it was, in fact, at an altitude higher than the top of Mount Snowdon (3,687 feet as against 3,560). Although the latitude was much the same as in his English home, he found the climate much harsher, exposed as the province of Alberta is to winds sweeping straight down from the Arctic. He notes at times that the temperature is down to $-38°F$ as early as November and that snow normally lies on the ground for months. Then in summer the continental heat is often combined with severe droughts. On the other hand, in seasons when the weather was favourable, his soil produced good wheat harvests. Nostalgically he sends back home for roots of some of the dainty woodland flowers he loved as a child. He has some success in establishing wood violets, though of the non-scented varieties, but none with primroses. After two or three years one of his primrose plants produced two stunted flowers.

His first house was evidently built of logs, and later he did a good deal of log-hauling for houses for neighbours. A Canadian researcher, investigating the early history of the Nose Creek settlements some thirty or so years ago, notes that he was ' ... a surveyor and went with many of the new homesteaders and helped them to locate their land'. That ties in well with James's avowed intentions on emigrating to Canada. *The Nose Creek Story, from 1792* was prepared and written by members of the community and was printed by John D. McAra Ltd of Calgary in about 1960.

Foremost in his vision of Empire was a Canada extending from Atlantic to Pacific, peopled with good, sound English stock. Ideally some of the stock would have been of his own breeding, but he accepted that he would be childless. Therefore he accepted the second-best alternative, of bringing to the new land young people of the families he knew well, many of them related to him or his wife. As soon as he felt he was sufficiently well established on his farm, he began writing letters to friends in 'the Old Country', particularly in Farley, Pitton and Winterslow, inviting them to come and try their luck in Canada. He had a well-thought-out programme. They were to come straight to his farm and stay there, helping with whatever there was to be done, until they felt confident enough to branch out on their own.

The scheme was outstandingly successful. From about 1890 onwards he coaxed at least seventy or eighty young people to venture. He kept no records – at least, none that have survived – but in the First World War families in our three villages were able to renew friendship with numbers of Canadian soldiers who were 'Uncle Jim's boys'.

Shortly before that war, in the autumn of 1912, James and Phillida paid a return visit to Britain. Apparently they made Farley their base but spent a good deal of time in

Pitton and Winterslow. Ted and his wife Alice were then living in the cottage that was later expanded into White Hill Farmhouse, as they had been ever since their marriage in 1901, and Ted's mother, Jane, and his sister, Kate, were occupying White Hill Cottage, a stone's-throw farther up the hill. In his subsequent letters from Canada James writes frequently and nostalgically of his memories of their visit, of the old friends they met and of the cascades of vividly coloured berries on the trees and bushes overhanging the chalk cliffs opposite.

James had a particular motive for this visit. He wanted to persuade Ted to emigrate to Canada and inherit the farmstead he had developed there. He might well have done so but for certain bonds which proved more powerful.

In that same year the Earl of Ilchester, an absentee landlord, had sold his Pitton and Farley estates. As related in *The Lost Village*, six of the small tenant farmers had approached the Wiltshire County Council with a request that it should invest in some of the land and let it to them, as it was empowered to do under the 1910 Smallholdings Act. With Ted acting as spokesman for the others, the scheme was approved and the transaction concluded. So a few months before James and Phillida arrived in Britain, Ted had at last realized his ambition and become a farmer. His share was ninety acres of bare land – a mile out of the village, it is true, but good, level land capable of improvement. Ted's mind was full of plans as to how he would develop it. A year earlier he might have been tempted to pull up his roots and trek to Canada, but not now.

Another major factor was the tie with the previous generations, notably Ted's mother, Jane, and Alice's father and mother, all growing old. Jane in particular was largely dependent on her only son, who naturally felt responsible for her, after her desperate struggle in his early years. Ted did indeed sound her on the idea of emigrating to Canada, to be met, as he expected, with an indignant, 'What! Leave Pitton! I wouldn't think of it! You can go if you like. I'm staying here!' So Ted, with a sigh, turned his back on a future in Canada.

James was naturally disappointed. Ted was, after all, his nearest surviving relation, the only nephew of his beloved wife. He would have liked nothing better than to see Ted settled on the Calgary farm and playing his part in the growth of that great Empire of which he had such an impelling vision. But Phillida was more pragmatic. She knew that it would never have worked out.

During the visit it became evident to Alice and Kate, if not to Ted, that Jane and Phillida did not like each other. Veiled hints and criticisms flew across the table at meal-times. Ted, his mind fixed on more solid matters, did not notice them, but Alice and Kate did. Religion seemed to be involved, for on Sundays Phillida refused to accompany the rest of the family to chapel.

When, before Christmas, James and Phillida departed, James gave Ted £100.

'It will help you to get your little farm going,' he said sadly. 'If only you could have come back with us, you could have had the lot.'

That evening Alice consoled the still doubtful Ted: 'Never mind! We'll make a success of what we're doing here!'

On a summer day in 1967 a car drew up at the author's door and decanted onto the garden path an elderly lady with a Canadian accent and a little old man in a vivid red shirt, cowboy leggings held up by a silver-buckled belt, and a ten-gallon hat. He was, he said, Edward Parsons, the adopted son of James Parsons of Calgary.

Sitting in an armchair, the old man delved into the past. He was almost blind and had been since infancy. James and Phillida had adopted him but had not been very kind to him. James used to humiliate him by carrying on conversations as though he were not there. Sometimes he would taunt him with his blindness.

James was not a good farmer, according to Edward. Everything had to be done his way or not at all. In spite of his visions of the future, he would not accept modern ideas and techniques. He was always behindhand with his work, and his crops were poor. The lads whom he persuaded to come out from Britain soon got fed up with living with Uncle James and putting up with his autocratic ways, and so they moved on.

He became disillusioned with his literary work and burned a lot of his manuscripts in one of his periodic clear-outs. He wrote nothing more, apart from his lengthy letters back to Britain. Once he destroyed a whole batch of letters with early Canadian stamps and took no notice of objections that they might be valuable. The farm was acquired eventually by Calgary Airport but was of poor quality and therefore fetched comparatively little. The £100 which James gave to Ted in 1912 probably represented his entire fortune at that date. There was little left for Edward when his adopted father died.

Perhaps because he was nearly blind, Edward Parsons had a phenomenal memory. Evidently conversation in James's house had been predominantly about the Old Country. Although Edward had never previously been to Britain, he had a vast store of information about Pitton, Farley and Winterslow. He produced some photographs of old Pitton worthies and proceeded to identify each portrayed, from their positions in the photographs, though he could not discern their faces. They had, of course, died years ago, but he could recite facts about each one, stating what they did and where they lived.

Eventually he came to Daniel Whitlock, whom his hearers realized, with a start, was Ted's father, to whose death so much mystery was attached. Were they going to hear the answer to that nagging query: Did Daniel go to hell or did he make it to heaven after all?

They were.

Daniel was Phillida's much-loved only brother, and he suffered from epilepsy. One can visualize the household, with old William Whitlock torn between the demands of his first family and of his second wife with a brood of small children. Hints of friction between the stepmother and her three stepchildren, Daniel, Phillida and Susannah, have survived. These three older ones would naturally have developed a bond between them, especially as Dan was delicate.

Dan was a lively lad, who played a cornet in the village band and enjoyed his glass of beer at the New Inn. When the strong-willed Jane Noyce of Winterslow married him, she undertook an uphill task, leading him into the straight and narrow path of Methodism and Temperance which she had adopted with enthusiasm when in domestic service in London. Eventually she had some success. Dan renounced the pub, took to going to chapel and even attempted to be a preacher. But the price of success was constant vigilance. Dan needed constant watching or he tended to become a backslider, as happened once or twice.

One market day in Salisbury Dan fell down in the street with an epileptic fit. He was picked up and carried into a house, where someone gave him a dose of brandy. Eventually he was identified as a Pitton man, so he was carried to the William IV Inn in Milford Street and propped up in the Pitton carrier's van, that being the depot for Pitton.

When the carrier returned, he thought Dan, whom he of course recognized, was drunk. The van lumbered along on its painfully slow journey to Pitton and when, 2½ hours later, it arrived at the village, Dan was still semi-conscious. The carrier and the other passengers were still under the impression that they had a drunken man to deal with. Laughing, they bundled him out at the corner in the middle of the village, where he rolled over and lay on the wet grass. It was raining.

Someone must have carried a message to Jane, who came down to the corner to investigate. Suspicious, she bent over him and smelt his breath. It reeked of brandy. Ashamed, disgusted and indignant, she turned away. He could stay there and sleep off his drunken stupor.

It was an hour or more before he came stumbling up the hill to his home. Jane heard his faltering step and thought she recognized it as being identical with what used to happen when he was a regular visitor to the New Inn. He staggered upstairs without a word, and within a few days he had died of pneumonia, brought on by exposure.

Poor Jane! She had allowed him to die of neglect.

Of course, she could never admit it. Her neighbours knew but she held aloof from them. She had made up her mind.

Dan was drunk. Drink had killed him. Her fanaticism

for the cause of total abstinence became stronger than ever.
She even emptied from its jar an innocuous little ginger-
beer plant, lest the drink it produced should be alcoholic.

No wonder that whenever Ted questioned his Uncle
Arthur or other villagers about the death of his father they
would say only, 'You must ask your mother about that.'
They knew, but did not want to stir up further trouble.

Aunt Phillida knew, too, and was not averse to saying so,
but by the time Ted was old enough to ask persistent
questions, Aunt Phillida was safely in Canada. Over there,
however, her adopted son averred that she developed a
bitter resentment against Methodism and teetotallers and
against her sister-in-law Jane in particular.

How sad to think of Jane and her orphaned children. All
those hardships; all the misery; the shadow of the workhouse; the desperate poverty; the humiliation of being a
pauper; the incessant work; the loneliness – all so unneces-
sary, after all. No wonder she couldn't face up to the truth
that it was her own fault. That would have been too great a
burden to bear.

That Jane was adamant about refusing to emigrate to
Canada is understandable. How could she go to live with
Phillida, knowing Phillida's opinion of the affair? She
would live out her life in the village that was her home,
where at least the neighbours would allow her to keep her
illusions, no matter what their private thoughts.

It says much for the innate compassion of those
nineteenth-century villagers that none of them ever
enlightened Ted about the facts of his father's death. He
died in his ninetieth year, still believing his mother's
version of the story. She sometimes used to tell Ted, 'I've
prayed about your father, and I believe he has gone to
heaven, after all.' Did she ever realize that so much of her
own life was a hell of her own making?

In the end she settled down to an evening of comparative
contentment. She saw her son building up a successful
farm, happily married and developing into a powerful
chapel preacher. She even in her last year saw her first
grandson. No doubt she was profoundly thankful when
the unwelcome visit of James and Phillida came to an end.

As for James, he seems to have been an even more

controversial character than Jane. At least she had the merit of consistency. But what *was* James?

A man of impressive vision? Yes, it took him far from his native meadows and lanes to help in the laying of the foundations of a great new fatherland for the English race. But when he got there, he apparently failed in the practical side of the task he set himself – to accept his son Edward's assessment.

A man of considerable literary ability? Yes, his editor in Britain and Edward Slow, the poet, had high opinions of his ability, as a young man. But when in his maturity he had the chance to develop his gifts, he shut the lid on them. In Canada he seems to have written virtually nothing, except those long letters home. These show some glimpses of genius but tend to be verbose and rambling.

An altruistic philanthropist? Yes, he did a great work in persuading young emigrants to leave home to people the empty lands of Canada, but Edward testified that when they arrived at his Calgary homestead they couldn't stand his autocratic ways and soon moved on.

A fine citizen? The historian of Nose Creek, Calgary, states that James was a local preacher and interested in church and all Sunday School work. 'Their door was always open to all comers.' Yet back in Britain he was reckoned 'an extreme radical agnostic'. And how do we reconcile his church activities with Phillida's irreconcilable prejudice against Methodists and Temperance advocates?

An enigma. A tormented, eccentric genius, maybe, as so many geniuses are. At least at the age of thirty-six he had the courage to follow his vision those many thousands of miles into a strange land.

In 1912, when he was giving Ted Whitlock the £100 he had brought with him, he said sadly:

'I had hoped for more than this. Once, long ago, the good Lord told me that if, like Abraham, I would leave my native land and journey to another, to which He would guide me, He would raise up from my family a leader who would, in some future time of trouble, rally the nations to Him and direct them into the paths of peace.

'I took it that this would be one of your descendants, Ted, and it is a disappointment to me that you turn your back on it. Perhaps, though, it is someone stemming from those whom I have brought to Canada over the past twenty-five years. Who knows?'

Ted was so impressed that he raised the question once more with his family. Ought they to go, after all?

Jane was contemptuous: 'It's my belief that the good Lord never told *him anything*! It's just his imagination running away with him.'

Oddly enough, Ted now has three great-grandchildren growing up on the Pacific coast of America – two in British Columbia and one in California.

Who knows?

Sources and Acknowledgements

The author gratefully acknowledges the generous grant made by The Author's Foundation towards research expenses, particularly regarding the chapter relating to Canada.

Extensive use was made of documents relating to Pitton and Farley in the Wiltshire County Archives. The author's best thanks are due to Mr Ken Rogers for his courtesy in helping with the selection and arranging the photo-copying. The relevant documents included the schedules and maps of the 1810 enclosure for the parish (note: the enclosure is dated 1810, though the maps bear the date 1819), and the tithe award map and schedule for the parish, dated 1838.

A major source of information regarding the rising of 1830 has been the *Salisbury and Winchester Journal* for that year and 1831, with subsidiary items from *The Times* of those years.

Use has also been made of petty sessions records for Salisbury and Amesbury in the mid-nineteenth century.

The Women's Institute Scrapbooks for Winterslow, Alderbury and Landford and Hamptworth are mines of information and reminiscences.

The author has been fortunate in having at his disposal

sundry handwritten documents, including diaries, memoirs, reminiscences and letters, notably those by the hands of Edwin Whitlock, Emmanuel Parsons, James Parsons and Helen Fry; he is indebted to Mr Chris Walker for permission to borrow and use Emmanuel Parsons' diaries. He extends his grateful thanks to J. Fitzgerald Moore of Calgary, who has provided important background information, supplementing *James Parsons' Letters*, on James Parsons' career in Canada, including extracts from *The Nose Creek Story*.

A general list of books of which considerable use has been made includes:

Agricultural Historical Review (ongoing, various publications)

Anstruther, Ian, *The Scandal of Andover Workhouse* (1973)

Beeton, Mrs, *Household Management* (first edition, 1859)

Brown, Martyn, *Australia Bound* (1988)

Bryant, Sir Arthur, *History of England* (1945)

Chafin, William, *Anecdotes & History of Cranbourn Chase* (1818)

Chandler, John, *Studying Wiltshire* (1982)

Christian, Garth, *A Victorian Poacher*, John Hawker's Journal (1969)

Clark, Manning, *Select Documents in Australian History* (1950)

Cobbett, William, *Rural Rides* (1851)

Colt-Hoare, Sir Richard, *Modern History of South Wiltshire* (1822–44)

Cox, J. Stevens, *A History of Ilchester* (1958)

Crabbe, George, *The Parish Workhouse*

Crowther, M.A., *The Workhouse System, 1834–1929* (1981)

Cunliffe, Dr Barry, *Danebury* (1983)

Davis, Thomas, *A General View of the Agriculture of Wiltshire* (1811)

Duck, Stephen, *The Thresher's Labour*

Eden, The Hon. Eleanor, *The Autobiography of a Working Man* (c.1840)

Fussell, G.F., *More Old English Farming Books* (1950)

Girouard, Mark, *Life in the English Country House* (1978)

Hammond, J.L. and Barbara, *The Village Labourer* (1911)

Hazlitt, William, *Essays*
Hopkins, Harry *The Long Affray (1985)*
Jefferies, Richard, *Round About a Great Estate* (1881)
Kerridge, Eric, *The Agricultural Revolution* (1867)
Minchinton, W.F., ed., *Essays in Agrarian History* (British Agricultural History Society) (1968)
Parsons, Michael, *Pitton & Farley* (1988)
Seebohm, M.E., *The Evolution of the English Farm* (1952)
Slow, Edward, *Wiltshire Rhymes* (1890s)
Stratton, J.M., *Agricultural Records* (1969)
Trevelyan, Professor G.M., *English Social History (1944)*
Trow-Smith, Robert, *English Husbandry*, (1951)
Vesey-Fitzgerald, Brian, *It's My Delight* (1947)
Young, Arthur, *A Tour through the Southern Counties* (1768)

The author has also made extensive use of his previously published work, both articles and books, including the following:
The English Farm
Historic Forests of England
Peasant's Heritage
A Short History of Farming in Britain
Wiltshire
The Folklore of Wiltshire
Salisbury Plain
The Shaping of the English Countryside

Index

Africa, 133
Ainsworth, Mrs, 134
Alberta, 206
Alfred the Great, 36
Alderbury, 11, 22, 76, 77, 101, 112, 117, 118, 174
Alderson, Mr Justice, 102, 104, 108, 109
Allotment Act, 69
America, 132, 133, 135, 155, 191, 192, 197, 214
Amesbury, 23, 149
Andover, 95, 99–113, 122, 123, 124, 125, 131
Anglo-Saxon Chronicle, 23
Animals, wild, 87
Anna Valley, 95, 99
Arthur, Col. George, 111
Australia, 102, 111, 129, 132, 133, 134, 135, 155, 205
Avon, R., 22, 24, 91, 105, 128, 182
Aylmer's Pond, 21

Baring, Bingham, 109
Barnett, James, 195–6
Bathurst, Sir Frederick, 148, 149–50
Batten, Mary, 195, 197
Baugh, Morris, 51
Baugh, William, 197
Beeton, Mrs, 148
Berkshire, 102
Birds, 85, 86, 182, 183
Bishopdown Farm, 99, 115, 204
Black Act, The, 57
Black Barn, The, 117
Black Lane, 66
Blackwood's Magazine, 124, 125
Bonnie Prince Charlie, 50

Boscobel Oak, 16
Botany Bay, 129
Bottom Way, 38, 66, 69, 144, 145
Boulter, Thomas, 142, 143
Bourne, R., 99, 101
Bourne Valley, 99, 101
Bournemouth , 133
Bowers Farm, 67, 113
Bradford-on-Avon, 83
Bridport, 16
Brieant Family, 154, 155, 191–2
Brighton, 17
Bristol, 11
Britford, 43, 44, 45
British Columbia, 214
British Empire, 205
Broughton, 101, 112, 196
Brown, Capability, 55
Bullington, 106, 114
Bustards, 182

Calgary, 204, 206, 207, 209, 210, 213
California, 214
Canada, 12, 129, 132, 133, 135, 155, 204–14
Chafyn, William, 82, 83, 182
Charles II, 15–19, 49, 59, 78, 92
Chicago, 133
Chilmark, 99
Christchurch & Harbour, 26, 101
Church Copse, 33
Churchwardens' Accounts, 48
Chute, 131
Clarendon, 18, 24, 33, 75, 76, 77, 78, 80, 101, 142, 148, 149
Clerkenwell, 140
Cobbett, William, 83, 91, 106, 107, 114, 128, 129, 182